FROM PARATROOPER TO PUBLIC DEFENDER

Reflections of a 103-year-old World War II veteran

By MORTON KATZ

Connecticut Chief Justice Richard A. Richard A. Robinson presents Morton Katz with a straw hat shortly before his 100th birthday. Morton was born on Straw Hat Day, May 15, in 1919. *Patrick Raycraft for the Hartford Courant*

FROM PARATROOPER TO PUBLIC DEFENDER

*To Shirley,
Rachel and Naomi*

FROM PARATROOPER TO PUBLIC DEFENDER

©Copyright 2023, Morton N. Katz, all rights reserved. Please contact the author or publisher for information about excerpts.

ISBN 978-0-9969602-1-2

Published by
Chi Chi Press
860-505-0482
860-538-3161
877-711-8265

FROM PARATROOPER TO PUBLIC DEFENDER

Contents

Chapter 1: The Parachute Tower 5

Chapter 2: ROTC 7

Chapter 3: Jump School 9

Chapter 4: Feet of Clay 12

Chapter 5: "You're Not Supposed to Be Here!" 13

Chapter 6: No Hope for the 509th 18

Chapter 7: "I Know Lawyer Abe Katz" 22

Chapter 8: A Late Thanksgiving 26

Chapter 9: Anzio 46

Chapter 10: A Holiday Service 51

Chapter 11: Maurice Rose: My Kind of General 53

Chapter 12: Close Call at Sadzot 55

Chapter 13: The Concentration Camp 60

Chapter 14: Descendent of Aaron 64

Chapter 15: Coming Home 66

History of the 509th Parachute Infantry Battalion 72

Letter to Eileen 80

Bibliography 92

Chapter 1: The Parachute Tower

I was born in 1919, ten years before the stock market crash and the beginning of the Great Depression. My father was a lawyer, but his practice was in real estate and few people were buying houses, so his practice went down the tubes and we lost our home. This, however, resulted in my first experience of somebody helping you out, although I was too young to know it at the time.

My father, Abe Katz, had a mortgage with a bank in downtown Hartford that went under. When a bank that's chartered by the state fails, it goes into receivership and the receiver is the state banking commissioner. As the banking commissioner was going through the paperwork, he came across our mortgage. He knew my father, and he did several things. First, he let us stay in the house without having to pay a per diem. Then he came to see my father. He was a wealthy man, and he gave my father a blank, signed check. He said use what you need, and when you're back on your feet you can pay me back at your convenience, and there's no interest involved.

Luckily, my father got a job with the Works Public Administration doing legal work, and my grandparents helped my parents get another house.

When I was in high school I wanted to go to West Point. My father was very close to our member of Congress, Herman Koppel, and I probably would have been accepted, but my parents didn't want me to go. I went to Connecticut State College instead.

One weekend I went to New York City. The 1939 World's Fair was in full swing. I had been on my college newspaper and had a little press card, so I thought maybe I could finagle my way in for free. When I showed my press card, to my surprise, a nice lady went over to a cabinet and came back with a big national press card and a strip of tickets. She said, "Have a good time." So I'm wandering around the World's Fair and who do I see but my kid brother, who was going to the Citadel at the time.

We wandered around the fair and went on some of the rides, and then we came to the Parachute Tower.

This was a 250-foot steel tower. At the top are four arms, and at the end of each arm there's a steel cable. So you'd get in this basket, and they'd strap you in. Then they'd take you up 250 feet, and there was some apparatus at the top which, the minute you hit the top, would let the basket drop. The parachute would deploy as you came down.

"Wow, let's take a ride on it," my brother said.

"Are you out of your mind?" I said. "Are you some kind of a nut?"

And then I said the famous words, which I would eat some time later: "You'll never get me on that damn contraption!"

The Parachute Tower at the 1939 World's Fair.
Pinterest

Chapter 2: ROTC

Connecticut State College is now the University of Connecticut. Being that it was a land grant college, ROTC was compulsory during the first two years.[1] I did very well in ROTC and wanted to take advanced ROTC, but I was majoring in chemistry and the science labs took priority over the outdoor training.

A friend got me into another program called CMTC, which stood for Citizens Military Training Camp. I remember seeing the placards advertising them on the buses and trolleys. The CMTC was one month a year for four years, and I went to Fort Devens in Massachusetts, which was an infantry training base.

The training was Mickey Mouse stuff. They didn't know what they were doing. The instructors were mostly retread World War I Reserve officers. I've seen better training in a sandbox. And I got commissioned as a second lieutenant. Since I wasn't working, I tried to get some active duty. The Army was just expanding, and I applied for what would become the first ski troops. I also applied for non-flight duty to the Air Corps, cargo duty aboard Army cargo ships, things like that. At the same time, an uncle suggested I go to Iowa State College and work toward a graduate degree.

Some money had been set aside for my education and my father's family was holding onto it, but one of his relatives blew it on a business venture. One of my mother's younger sisters met a gentleman from Belgium who was a chemist and was working for a big oil company. He put me through school at Iowa State.

---

[1] The Land Grant College Act of 1862, also known as the Morrill Act, gave federal land to the states to sell for the purpose of establishing colleges.

This was the second example in my life of somebody helping without seeking something in return.

My first year at Iowa State, from September 1940 into 1941, I was on scholastic probation. I was not a very good student. So I took the summer off and spent some time as a lifeguard in the borscht belt. I went back to school in the fall.

One day I got a call from from the sergeant major at the Old Post Office Building in Hartford, where a lot of the military recruiting stations were located. He said, "Would you like to have 21 days of active duty in Rhode Island?" I said yes.

The active duty was with the unit that was training the CMTC, and apparently somebody had ordered these tropical hats, like Doctor Livingston I presume, and we had to buy them most likely because the guy overbought them at the PX.

On December 7, 1941, I was attending a meeting at the student union at Iowa State. It was the first year that they had these portable AM radios, like a little Sony radio today. I saw some students gathered around it, and I asked them, "What's going on?"

"Pearl Harbor just got bombed."

I went right back to my rooming house and took my uniform down and polished the brass. I had orders within four days that I was to report in April to Fort Benning.

One thing that the Army did, it realized that the Reserve training up to that point was pretty pathetic. They sent all the Reserve officers that were called up to the school of their branch, and I got sent to the infantry school. I reported there in April of 1942.

Chapter 3: Jump School

While I was at Fort Benning, a pair of officers conducted a recruiting session for the Parachute School. At the end of the evening everyone was asked to sign an attendance sheet. Needless to say, anyone who signed the sheet learned that he had "volunteered" for the jump course. So I graduated from the infantry school in July 1942 and then went to the parachute school. Upon graduating in August of 1942 I was assigned to Company I, 3rd Battalion of the 502nd Parachute Infantry.

The 502nd at that time was a separate regiment, in the Alabama training area. We had about six weeks of training. It was all physical training in the morning, and in the afternoon you went to the parachute packing shed and learned how to pack the parachute, because you packed your own parachute for the jumps.

The physical training was rigorous. At one point I had been running, and then they had me as the first guy on the line for the rope climbing, and I was beat. I was down on my socks. We had to do a run after that and I started falling apart. A couple of GIs came up behind me and grabbed my elbows and I finished the run. And I said, "I just want you guys to know, I won't let you down."

Also, they made the officers train with the enlisted men. The idea was that when you got to the last point, where you're going to jump, you would be shamed into it. It was good psychology.

My first jump was surprisingly easy, because you were worked up to it psychologically. In the morning you would run a mile, and you'd have all kinds of physical training. You'd be jumping out of a box like a door on the airplane. You'd go down there and you'd be on a pulley, a harness, and it got to the point where you were no longer thinking about the jump, but you were doing all this training which was going to lead to the jump.

I don't think anybody in my class refused to jump. The first jump is the easiest. Then about the third or fourth jump you start to think, What the hell am I doing here?

We also had a couple of night jumps with the regiment. They dropped some guys in the river one night, and I think one of them drowned.

Overall, the training was very disorganized. I asked one of the officers above me, "When do we get some training in marksmanship?" He said "Mind your own business."

At that time, we didn't know it but they were planning the North African invasion. There was a battalion already in England with a lieutenant colonel, Edson D. Raff. Edson was a short, not dumpy, but unprepossessing guy. Raff, incidentally, became the commander who jumped in both the first and the last American airborne invasions of the war. He was a hell of a guy.

Then they sent us to Fort Bragg from Fort Benning to form the 101st Airborne Division. There I met Major General William C. Lee, who was known as the Father of the Airborne. He was in his fifties and had all kinds of injuries from jumping.

After the regiment was at Fort Bragg for about a week, all second lieutenants were ordered to report to regimental headquarters. Twelve of the lieutenants, including me, and 160 privates were to be sent to England as replacements. Raff was already in England with the 2nd Battalion of the 503rd, which was redesignated as the 509th Parachute Infantry Regiment prior to its first combat jump.

In those days things were pretty disorganized. We were not a unit going over, but were a "package" of replacements, and they had nothing like a "bring this, don't bring that" list. At least I had enough sense to sit down and think, and I sent home my Stetson hat, which I still have. A genuine original Army Stetson, which was part of the uniform you wore when you were commissioned in the advanced ROTC.

Also, the top two men in the ROTC training were given the Marine Corps option. A friend of mine, Eddie Finn, took the option, and he had a spectacular career in the Marines. He turned over all of his stuff to me, including his dress saber, because it

FROM PARATROOPER TO PUBLIC DEFENDER

was a different uniform. The saber, incidentally, is now in a display case with my daughter in Pennsylvania.

Paratroopers exit a mock fuselage on the morning before a practice jump.
Signal Corps photo / CCSU / Veterans History Project

Chapter 4: Feet of Clay

I went overseas on what was at that time the new Queen Elizabeth, the one that burned and sank in Hong Kong Harbor in 1972. Before we left, we were able to get passes. We were told that if we went to New York, we had to take off our wings, because somebody might see the wings and conclude that there are airborne troops.

We were in the last stages before departing and we knew it, so we worked out a deal where they told us "you can go home provided you're not more than 500 miles away, and you're going to sign this paper that you understand, when you come back, you don't take the last train from where you are, you're going to take the third from the last, and don't gamble on the train getting you back here on time. If you miss the boat, you'll be given a general court martial." Needless to say, five guys missed the boat.

During this time, my sister got me a date in New Jersey. Hotels were building these nightclubs in the front lobby so they could get people in and out fast. We got a table right out in front, very nice, and sitting at the table next to us was none other than Babe Ruth.

Now, you have to understand, Babe Ruth was one of the most revered figures in America. He's a married man with a family. He's larger than life, and kids would walk for miles just to go to a ballgame if they could get in and get his autograph. I'm not a kid, I'm a commissioned officer with responsibilities, but here is the idol of American youth, and he's at the next table stinking drunk, with six or eight floozies gathered around him. I could just see the statue up there with the feet turned to clay. It was so disillusioning.

Chapter 5: "You're Not Supposed to Be Here!"

The trip overseas was relatively uneventful. When we started out, they made us go below decks. The British crew would steal rations from the food on board for the troops. Then they would go down below decks, where the enlisted men had bunks five or six high, and they would sell sandwiches to the troops from their own food. We had the 29th Infantry Division on board, and finally the commanding general came down and said, "These guys are selling you your own food, and what you should do is take the sandwich and don't pay for it. What are they gonna do, sue you?"

In essence we were a package of a dozen very green, raw second lieutenants and 160 privates. We arrived in Scotland and boarded a train, which took us down to Chilton Foliat in Hungerford at the beginning of October 1942. When I reported to Lieutenant Colonel Raff, he said, "You're not supposed to be here!" He said we were to join him later in the combat zone.

We didn't know it at the time, but the battalion was preparing for Operation Torch, the airborne invasion of North Africa. The battalion, minus the package of replacements, which include me, went to the staging area and took off from Land's End on the night of November 7, 1942. This was the first American airborne operation of the war and the longest airborne invasion in history: 1,600 miles to Algeria.

They took off on the night of November 8. The radar didn't work, the navigation was lousy, and they got lost. The password didn't work. We met them later, and the guys had some tough operations.

The first trooper to be killed was Dave Kunkel, and we had some other losses. Bill Moir, the battalion surgeon, took a 20 millimeter shell in the back of his helmet. It sent splinters right through his skull, but he refused to be evacuated. He was out there all day operating under fire. He got the first Distinguished Service Cross to be awarded to an airborne medical officer. It may have been the first DSC to be awarded to any doctor in the war. He was eventually operated on and he survived, but we never saw him again.

The next week the main body jumped in an attempt to capture an airport, and one of the Air Corps officers with them was Colonel Philip Cochran. He was the model for the character Flip Corkin in the comic strip Terry and the Pirates.

They captured the airfield, and then they went on to take another area. The French unit there greeted them with open arms, and they got an order passed that came from their theater commander authorizing us to wear their badge. I've still got mine. And years later, the British trained them. We didn't get any of the British training because we came over just at the last minute. Lieutenant General Sir Frederick Browning, whose wife was the writer Daphne DuMaurier, got a list of as many officers as he could, and he sent each of us the red beret. I've still got mine, and wear it when I go to Memorial Day services.

Meanwhile, Raff was promoted to full colonel and was sent back to the States to form the 507th Parachute Infantry Regiment. He went on to take part in D-Day, and then he took part in Operation Varsity, which was the jump over the Rhine River.

We had some parachute training in Boufarik, Algeria. That's where the opera star Lily Pons was born. Later she and her husband, the famous pianist Jose Iturbi, gave a full concert in downtown Naples.

We had a trooper, Nicky DeGaeto, who was an operator. I don't know how he did it. One day he'd be in the motor pool. One day he'd be in the kitchen. One day he'd be somewhere else. So he finds out that we are on our way to Morocco, and he starts saving sugar and this and that. We get to Morocco, and he contacts a guy there that makes ice cream. No one really knows it. And we're having noon mess out on the desert floor, it's hot

FROM PARATROOPER TO PUBLIC DEFENDER

as hell. Suddenly we see this cloud of dust, and it's Nicky in a three quarter ton truck coming like hell. He comes up, and the truck's full of marmite cans, the big, thick vacuum cans, full of ice cream.

Our group still hadn't gone into combat. The only troopers who went into combat were the ones from our replacements, and the plane they were on was forced down. It ran out of gas in Spanish Morocco. A lot of this is in Raff's book, "We Jumped to Fight," and another book by General William P. Yarborough. Yarborough at the time was the liaison officer between Mark Clark's headquarters and the invasion forces. I didn't know him at the time, and all I ever saw of Raff was he more or less greeted us when we got to Chilton Foliat.

We went to Africa on the Borinquen, a Puerto Rican ship. We had about ten officers in our group by this time, and one of the guys wanted to be a wiseass. He said, "Oh, I'm sick." Everybody in our cabin was sick. Before we got under way I met a Navy ensign who was in charge of the gun crew on the ship, and he showed me how to avoid seasickness. Very simple. You get up on deck and you go fore, aft, topside, down. Always walk in different directions and keep it up. I didn't get seasick. I ate like a king on that ship. It was an easy trip, at least for me. The ensign wrote the book "Convoy to Murmansk," which was turned into a movie. He had no use for the Merchant Marine. They were always in the cargo. They'd chop off the corner of a box to look into it. They stole plenty. Among the things we had with us going in to Africa was our uniforms, and what uniforms they couldn't use, they cut them with an X across the back.

We got to Africa, and it was disorganized to beat hell. We marched all the way up from the pier to the railroad station to wait for orders. I've got a funny story about that. The French had sabotaged the airfield, and they had smashed up what was not damaged in combat. And one of the things they smashed were the typewriters.

We were all given cards to be mailed by the Red Cross, saying "Am safe and well, Somewhere in North Africa." It happened that there were three or four guys in our group of replacements

FROM PARATROOPER TO PUBLIC DEFENDER

who had worked at Royal and Underwood. They had the typewriters up and working in a couple of hours. The American soldier would improvise; he was resourceful as hell.

I was out in the field one night. The airstrip was still in good shape, and a Lockheed Lightning comes in and makes a nice, smooth landing. It comes to a stop and I see the hatch pop open. This young pilot gets out and he's wearing a Class A uniform. He takes off his flight helmet and puts on his crush hat, the 50 mission crush hat, and he's wearing a shirt and tie, paisley greens. He gets out of the plane and he comes over and says, "Hey buddy, where's the officers club?" It was hysterical.

A similar thing happened months later. We were in Morocco, and they would send aircraft with cargo in them. So we're out there, and there's nothing there but sand and dirt. This C-47 comes down, and the pilot says "Hey, where's the Coke machine?"

In Boufarik, we were able to get some training material and a couple of C-47s, and we were doing some jump training. When I went out the door everything seemed to be all right, but I couldn't get my head up. The lines were all twisted. As I was going past the other paratroopers, they were yelling "Pull your reserve!" Which I did, and eventually the parachute opened. I was still descending pretty fast, and I realized that two of the panels became separated. I hit hard, but I was OK. Nicky DeGaeto, meanwhile, broke his leg on the practice jump. He said it ruined his dancing career. I said, "What career?"

No sooner had I gotten out of the faulty parachute than the rigging sergeant, L.C. MacLaney, came running over. "Lieutenant," he said, "you are jumping in the next stick. Here's your parachute. There's your airplane. Go." It's like falling off a horse or a bicycle. Immediately, you've got to go over and jump, so you can't have time to think about it.

When we all got transferred, MacLaney wound up as the chief rigger in the 82nd Airborne Division.

But I did think about it, much later on. When I was released from active duty, I started having dreams. I would dream that I'm floating and the damn parachute is not going to open.

FROM PARATROOPER TO PUBLIC DEFENDER

The dreams persisted until 1964, the year I got married. Within a short time after I was married, the dreams went away. Shirley just had some, I can't quite express the words, but there were no more nightmares.

Chapter 6: No Hope for the 509th

We found out that we were going to be part of the 5th Army. We started out at a little town called Maison Carrée, and there was a hotel there. We could at least go down to the bar and have a couple drinks. The closest I got to combat at that point, a bunch of us were going down to the hotel to have a couple drinks, we were going down this narrow alleyway and Bing! Someone took a shot at us. Luckily he was a lousy shot.

I still hadn't been assigned, so I was temporarily a mess officer. It was an easy job. All I did was I looked in the 201 files and I found guys who had been cooks in civilian life. So I got rid of the Southerners, all they did to cook was drop it in hot grease, and I had time to give our guys some training. There were sandbags around there, as well as sand dumps, so I got my guys up there and gave them some good hard training.

While we were there, the French Admiral Darlan was assassinated on Christmas Eve of 1942.[2] After the assassination, most of our battalion was called out to patrol the streets with submachine guns.

At the time we were staying in a school. The school was gone, but the woman who ran the school was still there. She didn't have time to get out, and her husband was trapped in occupied France.

The Americans figured, I think, that once they landed, the Germans were just going to melt away. And they weren't going to melt away. They were well trained. They had better equipment than we had. We had this crummy tank. Have you seen the movie "Sahara"? In the movie Humphrey Bogart is the tank

---

[2] Admiral Francois Darlan agreed to order all French forces in North Africa to cease resistance and cooperate with the Allies. He was assassinated by an anti-Vichyiste on Dec. 24, 1942.

commander of a medium tank, and the medium tank was a piece of crap. It had a gun on one side, so in order to shoot the gun forward you had to turn the tank around, and you made a bigger target of yourself. And we had gasoline in these flimsy five gallon metal cans, so we copied what the Germans had. They called it the jerry can, and it had three grips and a better metal casing. Then they had an entrenching tool where you just took the shovel, loosened the bolt, opened it up, and it became a pick. You'd go to the scene of a battle and you could smell the equipment burning. Our equipment was crap. At least we had the M-1 rifle, which was a damn good weapon.

One thing was clear: We needed more training. Raff was gone with the main body up in Tunisia. He ran a hell of an operation there. He only lost one man. But we had to learn the hard way. The Germans were very well trained. One thing was interesting, though. According to our intelligence reports, the famous German commander Erwin Rommel was probably the only German commander who stuck to the Geneva Convention. I'll give him credit for that.

And we had some amusing experiences. When spring came, we used to go to a little town inside Algeria and we played baseball against a hospital team. So we're down there one day, we finished the game, we're packing up, and this youngster comes over. He gets to talking, and people always do this when they ask this question, I had told him we're here to play baseball, and they do this sort of sideways, "Are you Jewish?"

I said "Hell, yes."

He said, "Would you like to go to a seder?"

I said yes.

So he gives me directions to his home, the date and time.

I had to make arrangements to get a jeep. It was a lot of work to get to go someplace if it wasn't official. So I get down there, I wore my khakis, and I find the house with no trouble at all. I ring the doorbell, there's no answer. I knock on the door, for a half, three-quarters of an hour. There was no one home, or if there was, they didn't respond. And I said the hell with it.

I started back, and the MPs stopped me. They said, "Lieutenant, you can't use that highway tonight because Arab marauders are out and you won't get anywhere alive." So I went back to the hospital and had dinner there, and they put me up for the night.

Boy, was I pissed. So we went down to play ball again two weeks later and the kid was there. I went over and said, "Good joke. You put one over on a stupid American lieutenant."

I was pretty sore, and his sister said, "Why are you harassing my brother?"

I told her what happened, and she said, "Ohh, there was supposed to be a gendarme there. The seder was changed to my grandmother's house." So she gave me the names of some Jewish people in Oujda, in Morocco, where we were, and I met a lot of great people there.

We were working our way west to Morocco to form the 5th Army, and one thing, we ate like kings. The 5th Army issued us some great rations. When we got there, the first ration we got was frozen Long Island duck. And our mess sergeant, John Frascina, was a professional chef and baker in civilian life. They told everybody that you can't make pies and cakes on the field range. We didn't know you can't. It was just a case of taking that big heavy cover and turning it upside down, and making a few adjustments in the heat. When we finally got to Belgium, General Ridgway took John to be his personal chef.

The next big thing that happened was that the 82nd Airborne Division came over. I cannot emphasize this enough. The 82nd Airborne Division did not, not, not participate in any combat whatsoever in North Africa. They got there in early May of 1943, by which time the fighting was over.

At that time the artillery commander for the 82nd Airborne, I forget his name, he eventually became Chief of Staff by the way, was upset because "we didn't get there first!" He got all bent out of shape. And the first thing that happened, we were cut off from the 5th Army, and we started getting rations that were issued by the division, and they were lousy. The second thing that happened was that Bob Hope did his first overseas show

FROM PARATROOPER TO PUBLIC DEFENDER

after we went into Tunisia with the 82nd Airborne Division, and they wouldn't let our guys, the 509th Parachute Infantry, go to the Bob Hope show. How childish can you get? But in their early publicity, the 82nd Airborne tried to get credit for combat service in North Africa. They did not fight in North Africa.

FROM PARATROOPER TO PUBLIC DEFENDER

Chapter 7: "I Know Lawyer Abe Katz"

We found out that we were going to be in reserve under the 82nd Airborne in the 325th Glider Regiment for the invasion of Sicily. The C-47s took off from a nearby field to drop the paratroopers, and I'll never forget, there was a young lieutenant from Brooklyn, and he was standing in the door of the plane when they took off, and his was one of the planes that got shot down by our own ships.[3]

General Ridgway, by the way, did not jump into Sicily. He made up for it, however, by jumping into Normandy, and the story is, some guys were suiting up and getting their gear on and one said, "If they're gonna make that poor old guy jump, I can jump."

I was busy at the time, and nothing was coordinated. I finally got into Sicily, and our unit was gone. I had verbal orders advising me that Ridgway had gotten permission from Clark to drop our people at Avellino, which was an important road junction.

Now this is another true story, and a funny one at that. Lieutenant Charles McKinney was one of the guys who came over in the next group, in the spring of '43. McKinney took a group of about half a platoon strength on patrol, and a civilian comes out of a house and yells "Don't shoot! I know President Roosevelt. I know Jim Farley. I know lawyer Abe Katz!"

That was my father's name.

So they took him back to our lines, got the information from him, and I wrote to my father. He writes back and says, "Yes, I know Mike. He was a bootlegger. He was convicted, and because

---

[3] Eighty-one paratroopers were killed and 132 wounded when planes carrying the 504th Regimental Combat Team were fired on by their own ships off the coast of Sicily, according to HistoryNet.

he was not a citizen, he was deported to Italy. He was my client." Years later, I was appointed a Superior Court magistrate and I was sitting on small claims cases; those are monetary cases only up to $5,000. And I was also doing infractions, things like speeding. I could take away your license but I couldn't put you in jail. And I loved it; that was a lot of fun. One day I was hearing small claims in Manchester and a plaintiff failed to appear. When I dismissed the case for the defendant, his name, DeFeo, seemed familiar. I told the defendant the story about Mike DeFeo, and he said, "Yes, he was my cousin."

At any rate, back in Sicily, I got everything all organized. I'm working without any written orders, and I had to get an LST to take us to Naples. And we found out that when the Nazis left Naples, they put a bomb in the post office, and when it went off it killed 125 civilians, mostly women and children.

In order to arrange for the LST, I had to go down to the Navy headquarters at Palermo. I had a jeep and a driver, and we were running low on gas, and we hadn't eaten all day. So we got to this area of supply depots, but there was a sign that said "No transients. Don't stop here. We won't feed you," etcetera. At the very bottom of the hill, there was a sign that said such and such quartermaster battalion. I didn't see anybody for a few moments. Then a couple of men came out, and I realized it was a segregated unit. I said to myself, why don't I do this by the book? So I went into the orderly room and an African American corporal was at the desk. I asked if I could see the commander. He said sure. So I went in and I saluted him. Then I spoke with him, and I called him Sir. And I said "Here's the situation. We're going to the Navy base. We're out of gas. We haven't eaten all day. We need a couple of things. Can you help us?" And he did. I thanked him, and when I left I saluted on my way out. You've got to start somewhere.

You know, I didn't believe it at first. I took the train from Hartford the night I was on my way to Fort Benning. In Washington, D.C., we transferred to a Southern Railroad train, and I see the conductor segregating the passenger cars. I didn't want to believe it at first. It was true. Then we get to Atlanta, and the signs are there: drinking fountains, white, colored. Waiting room, white, colored. A couple of paratroopers gave me a ride to Columbus, and then I took the bus into town. I got on the bus, and the same thing: white, colored.

I fnally got my people on the LST and we went into Naples. Naples, at that time, and most of the time anyway, was a den of thieves. The lanes were marked out with barbed wire on heavy posts, and they still lost cargo. So what you would do is, these trucks kept coming and going, so you'd grab a truck and say OK, you're my truck, and then we had to find out where the battalion was. It was at the top of the Via Roma, in the Ticino area.

So I get a truck, we load it with our stuff, and I had a couple of men in the body of the truck carrying rifles and I sat in the front seat with the driver and I have a .45 sticking out of the window. We're going as we're lined up, and I didn't know it, but the commander – the executive officer was in command at that time – had been lost, and he walked into a trap. He was captured, and I never saw him again. There was a new commander, William T. Yarborough, a great guy, and he was in the office.

"Lieutenant," he said, "you're my adjutant."

Well, the adjutant always goes with the commanding officer. So my first combat operation with Yarborough was on November 11, 1943, we took Mount Santa Croce in Onofro.

I had reported to Yarborough in the new headquarters on or about October 1, 1943, and they were already making plans to take the mountain. And the first thing I did, Yarborough took a personal reconnaissance, and he took me with him. I thought he was going to walk to Berlin, scared the heck out of me. But Yarborough was the kind of guy that if you were with him, you knew it would work out okay. He was a tremendous leader. He was one of the earlier people involved in the airborne operation.

On November 11, he led the advance up Mount Santa Croce. One of our original men was Pappy Curtis. He was from Maine. He tripped two bouncing betty mines – they would spring up before detonating – and didn't get a scratch. You have the trip wires. You have to hear the click. If you hear it, you hit the ground. He was one of the guys that came back to Connecticut.

FROM PARATROOPER TO PUBLIC DEFENDER

He worked in the aircraft industry, and I used to have mini-reunions at my home in Avon.

Chapter 8: A Late Thanksgiving

Thanksgiving of 1942 was approaching, and due to a miscalculation about how long the North African campaign would last, the supply system came up short. Thus we were authorized to obtain turkeys from the local economy, at 60 pounds per 100 men, at a cost of 60 cents a pound. I arranged with a local entrepreneur to raise the turkeys. The day before Thanksgiving, he came to me stating that the chief of police in "Sattarno" had confiscated the turkeys on the claim that they were being raised for the black market. He told me that the turkeys were "just down the road."

I took off with him in his alcohol burning truck, with only a soft cap, fatigue coveralls, a GI raincoat, "boondocker" work shoes, and carrying my Colt .45.

After a long haul, he pointed to a road marker, saying "There it is!" The road sign said "St. Arnaud 240 km." (This was the "Sattarno" to which he referred.) We kept driving and arrived in St. Arnaud late at night, after many stops to clean out the carburetor. The police chief apologized to me, but said he had already turned my turkeys over to the British, so there was no getting them back.

I spent the night at a local café drinking hot, sweet Turkish coffee. The café was like a Hollywood casting call with French Foreign Legionnaires, Arab Goumiers with tarbooshes (a green fez), and miscellaneous French soldiers and Arab civilians. I hitched a ride back to Maison Carrée with a very suspicious Army chaplain in a broken-down vehicle. He kept a beady eye on me until we arrived and the sentry saluted me.

The Thanksgiving turkeys finally did arrive – just in time for Christmas, and we served hot, roast stuffed turkey to the whole battalion. That night I was censoring mail, and one young trooper wrote home to his mother: "Mom, today we had roast stuffed turkey. I hate roast stuffed turkey." Years later my daughters would use this story as the basis of respective high school reports.

We were on Mount Santa Croce for about a month and a half. I became S-2, which is intelligence, for a short while, and I ran my own patrols, and sometimes went out with a patrol to bring back a prisoner. I had a young trooper with me, Dee Fisco. We were with Darby's Rangers. I remember coming back from a patrol and one of the Rangers said to me, "Nice job." I'd covered some hot stuff there. When he said "Nice job," I felt like I'd been given the DSC. Darby was a hell of a leader.

In early December we were relieved to prepare for the invasion of Anzio.

The Anzio beachhead, March 1944. *Morton Katz collection*

FROM PARATROOPER TO PUBLIC DEFENDER

Master Rigger, Tech Sgt. L.C. MacLaney of Hartford, Alabama, packs a parachute for Staff Sgt. C.E. Cole of San Angelo, Texas, at the 503rd Parachute Infantry Battalion training post in Hungerford, England, August 1942.
Signal Corps / CCSU / Veterans History Project

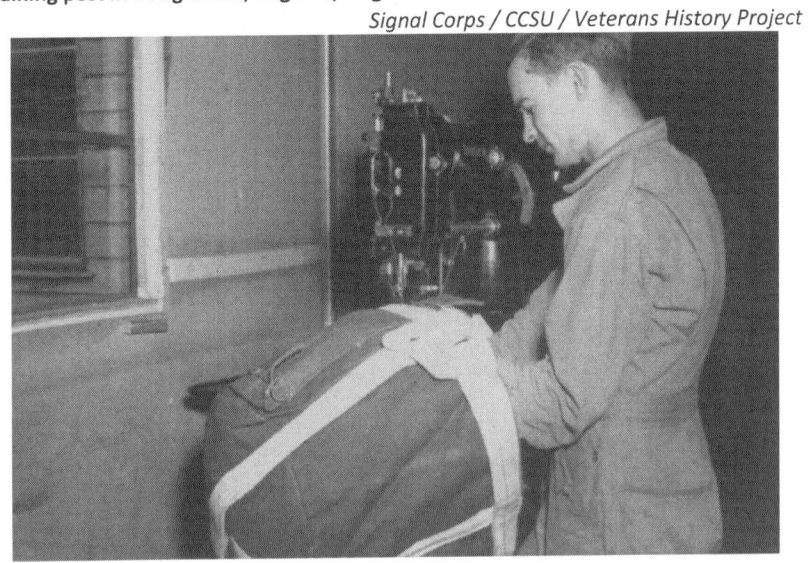

Colonel Monroe Wells mends a parachute in preparation for a practice jump in England. Signal Corps / *CCSU / Veterans History Project*

FROM PARATROOPER TO PUBLIC DEFENDER

Paratroopers board a C-47 for a training jump in Hungerford, England, in October 1942. *Signal Corps / CCSU / Veterans History Project*

Paratroopers load a jeep to take on maneuvers.
Signal Corps / CCSU / Veterans History Project

FROM PARATROOPER TO PUBLIC DEFENDER

Paratroopers await orders to jump during maneuvers in Hungerford, England, Oct. 2, 1942. *Signal Corps / CCSU / Veterans History Project*

Troopers land during the practice jump in England.
Signal Corps / CCSU / Veterans History Project

FROM PARATROOPER TO PUBLIC DEFENDER

And away we go. *Signal Corps / CCSU / Veterans History Project*

FROM PARATROOPER TO PUBLIC DEFENDER

Lieutenant Edmund J. Tomasik checks the equipment of the men on his planeload. Tomasik would go on to retire as a full colonel.
Signal Corps / CCSU / Veterans History Project

Lieutenant Fred Perry of Dayton, Ohio, inspects a reserve parachute before going on maneuvers. *Signal Corps / CCSU / Veterans History Project*

FROM PARATROOPER TO PUBLIC DEFENDER

Pfc. John Patton mends a strap before making a practice jump.
Signal Corps / CCSU / Veterans History Project

2nd Battalion, 509th Parachute Infantry Regiment, at Camp Kunkle, Oujda, French Morocco. Dave Kunkle was the first paratrooper to be killed.
Signal Corps / CCSU / Veterans History Project

FROM PARATROOPER TO PUBLIC DEFENDER

E Company, 509th Parachute Infantry Battalion, commanded by Captain Erven E. Boettner, in Oujda, North Africa. *Signal Corps / CCSU / Veterans History Project*

A fleet of DUKWs in assault formation head for the beach at Baia Bay on Jan. 14, 1944, in rehearsal for the Anzio landings.
Signal Corps / CCSU / Veterans History Project

Cpl. Marion W. Shade of Miamisburg, Ohio, left, and Tech Sgt. Lester C. McLaney prepare 2-inch mortar shells for dropping by parachute on Jan. 13, 1944, in Naples.
Signal Corps / CCSU / Veterans History Project

Sergeant McLaney wraps K rations for dropping as well.
Signal Corps / CCSU / Veterans History Project

FROM PARATROOPER TO PUBLIC DEFENDER

Morton Katz in Naples, Italy, spring 1944. *Morton Katz collection*

From left, Captain S.L. Newgate, commander of the Winchester Castle, Lt. Col. William P. Yarborough, C.O. of the 509th Parachute Infantry Battalion, and Lt. Col. Roy A. Murray, C.O. of the 4th Ranger Battalion, aboard the Winchester Castle study a model of the beach where troops will land.

Signal Corps / CCSU / Veterans History Project

FROM PARATROOPER TO PUBLIC DEFENDER

Itri, Italy, spring 1944. *Signal Corps / CCSU / Veterans History Project*

Buildings in Formia, Italy, spring 1944.
Signal Corps / CCSU / Veterans History Project

Cpl. Marion W. Shade and Tech Sgt. Lester C. McLaney packing medical supplies to be dropped by arachute, Naples, Jan. 13, 1944.

Signal Corps / CCSU / Veterans History Project

FROM PARATROOPER TO PUBLIC DEFENDER

Troopers of the 509th Parachute Infantry Battalion, 1st Airborne Task Force, during the invasion of Southern France. *Signal Corps / CCSU / Veterans History Project*

Tech Sgt. Lester McLaney, left, and Staff Sgt. Arthur E. Dickerson of Picayune, Miss., and Cpo. William D. Ates of Holt, Florida load supplies into an adapted P-40 auxiliary belly tank for advanced troops behind enemy lines in Italy, Naples, Jan. 13, 1944.
Signal Corps / CCSU / Veterans History Project

FROM PARATROOPER TO PUBLIC DEFENDER

From left, troopers McCall, Campbell, Morton Katz, Frederick, Tomasik, Pritchett, Oldham and Kelly receive awards at a ceremony. *Morton Katz collection*

Members of the 509th prepare to leave Born, Belgium on 22 January 1945 during the Battle of the Bulge. *Signal Corps / CCSU / Veterans History Project*

FROM PARATROOPER TO PUBLIC DEFENDER

Troopers of A Company, 509th, with soldiers of the 7th Armored Division (camouflaged in white) use a crude sled to bring a wounded soldier to an aid station, Born, Belgium, 21 January 1945. *Signal Corps / CCSU / Veterans History Project*

Germans who died when the 509th fought the 1st and 2nd Battalions of the 25th Panzergrenadier Division, 29 December, 1944.
Signal Corps / CCSU / Veterans History Project

FROM PARATROOPER TO PUBLIC DEFENDER

The 509th attends a USO show featuring jazz trumpeter Clyde McCoy in Piscinola, Italy, spring 1944.
Signal Corps / CCSU / Veterans History Project

Troopers of the 509th and the 7th Armored Division move toward enemy positions beyond St. Vith, Belgium, 24 January 1945.
Signal Corps / CCSU / Veterans History Project

FROM PARATROOPER TO PUBLIC DEFENDER

Morton Katz is flanked by Dennis Irvin and Ken Shaker at the Veterans Day Parade in New York City, Nov. 11, 1995. *Morton Katz collection*

Morton on Memorial Day in Formia, Italy, in 1944. *Morton Katz collection*

FROM PARATROOPER TO PUBLIC DEFENDER

Morton and Shirley Katz *Morton Katz collection*

Colonel Morton Katz with Connecticut Governor Ella Grasso and Shirley Katz, with the Katzes' two daughters, Naomi, left, and Rachel, on June 9, 1979.
Morton Katz collection

FROM PARATROOPER TO PUBLIC DEFENDER

The 2000 reunion of the 509th Parachute Infantry in Fayetteville, North Carolina *Morton Katz collection*

Company E, 509th Parachute Infantry Battalion, commanded by Captain Erven E. Boettner, in Oujda, North Africa.
Signal Corps/CCSU/Veterans History Project

Chapter 9: Anzio

They had some crazy idea of bringing in 105-millimeter guns in DUKWs (amphibious vehicles). I happened to be down there one day. They were rehearsing, and it didn't occur to anybody to determine the capacity of the DUKW and to get the weight of the gun. They started out on the first trial run, and everything sank.

We went to Anzio on a British ship, the HMS Winchester Castle. The British had some great rations. One of the things they were using was a ration for seven men for two days, or two men for seven days, or one man for 14 days. It was good, but for some reason, we couldn't use their rations.

They had other stuff that was not in our K rations. Good stuff, too. The prize was 28 bars of semisweet chocolate, Cadbury's. That's what we went for first.

Anzio should have been a great operation, but General Mark Clark, who was in charge of the operation, made a mistake. He told Major General John Lucas, who was the 6th Corps commander, to be cautious. Well, you don't be cautious in an amphibious operation. Get the hell on that beach and get the hell off it.

We hit the beach at 2 o'clock in the morning on the 22nd of January. I went right down on the beach. I was right with Yarborough in the first boat. And we went to the right and we knocked over the Nazis' Fascist headquarters, and gee, these guys had pumpernickel in big vacuum cans, big tubes of what looked like toothpaste, and high quality cheese.

I went up the stairway and I had to take a left turn, and the door was locked at the head of the stairs. So I had to do a John Wayne and I said "Okay, Fisco, let 'em have it." Dee Fisco blew the lock off with his submachine gun and I charged in with my .45 and a hand grenade at the ready. But the room was empty.

FROM PARATROOPER TO PUBLIC DEFENDER

In another room we found a map with the location of the mines on the beach, as well as a bottle of scotch and a Kodak Retina camera. I had a sergeant with me, and I asked him if he would prefer the camera or the scotch. He opted for the scotch. That camera served me well throughout the rest of the war, and I still have it.

One of my vivid recollections of the Anzio beachhead operation concerns an arrogant Nazi pilot, who was shot down over the beachhead. We interrogated him to learn the location of his airfield in order to have the Army Air Corps destroy it. He was very stubborn until I told my interrogator to tell the pilot who and what I was. He said to the pilot, "Der Oberleutnant ist ein Jude." (The lieutenant is a Jew.) Fearing for the consequences, the pilot gave us the location of the airfield, and the Air Corps took it from there.

We got as far as Turano, where the son of the Italian patriot Garibaldi is buried. We were making good time, when we got this crazy order to stop and dig in. I thought Yarborough was going to have a fit. He was really pissed. We were moving. Years later, I saw an interview with Field Marshal Albert Kesselring's chief of staff, and he said that if the Allies kept on going, we could have been in Rome the first day. But we had to stop, and we were bogged down on the beach. The Germans brought in their big guns, the heavy artillery, in the mountains on the other side of the beachhead, and we lost seven thousand men killed on that beach.

Clark was interviewed on that same channel sometime later, and he made some remark like "We had to consolidate the beachhead." Like hell you do.

At least one thing Clark did, in 1940 he came out with a field jacket, a flimsy thing, but when we got to the beachhead, it came in very handy. I still have mine, by the way.

There's a saying, the British fight for king and country, the Germans fight for the Fatherland, and the Americans fight for souvenirs. I never lost my steel helmet. I still have it. I have a jump suit I took home. I got a nice prize in Germany, a Rhine Metal Vorsig typewriter, all the exposed parts are chrome plated.

I thought it was packed very well but I guess it dropped off the crane or something. I left that on the pier in New York. I still have my Air Corps sleeping bag. I was issued one of the first new .45s, the A-1 with the arch housing. I had a bunch of boots. I gave one pair each to a couple of museums. I have two pair left. I'm going to give one to the state museum, and the other is an heirloom. It's not going anywhere.

When Colonel Raff told me "You're not supposed to be here," we had other replacements come in in the spring of 1943 as well, and we had a company left over. We called this the Parachute Scout Company, and Bill Howland was the commander. He was an unreconstructed Southerner. I didn't like him, but I respected him. We had a lot of arguments about religion and race.

Howland was very smart. He came up to the shore on a good-size boat and he had a white flag and an American flag, and he got the German commander down, and bluffed him into thinking we had an enormous task force on the way that would blow them out of the water. Which we didn't, of course. But they surrendered, without a shot being fired. Howland got the Legion of Merit for his leadership, and he certainly deserved it. Years later, Howland's widow was working for the government and they had a Reduction in Force, and she was about to lose her job. We found out that if we could get an affidavit that he was killed in action, it would save her job. That was easy for me, because Howland was killed right beside me.

Our staff officers were always up front, and one day we came under fire. I was standing next to Howland. A shell hit. I could feel the shell fragments hitting my steel helmet, and the blast knocked him down and killed him instantly. I gave her an affidavit and it saved her job. But there were times I thought this fellow Howland had a KKK bedsheet in his helmet.

The 509th Parachute Infantry Regiment spearheaded the breakout from the beachhead and we were sent to Ostia, on the west coast of Italy outside Rome. Years later a client of mine in Hartford told me he was there with the Italian army before the war. I sent some books we found there to my physics professor at UConn, and he got a big kick out of that.

We made some practice jumps while we were staging for Operation Dragoon, the invasion of Southern France. I met Joe Louis, who was in the area with the USO. He boxed some of the troops, but went easy on them so as not to embarrass them in front of their friends. I also met Irving Berlin at a bar in Rome. He was in Italy with his show "This is the Army."

Meanwhile, I still had not jumped in combat. The battalion was preparing for the invasion of Southern France, so I went to see the commanding officer. I said "Colonel, we're going into Southern France. As you know, because we weren't part of the plan, I didn't make the first two jumps in North Africa, and I was still in North Africa when we jumped into Sicily. Now we're coming into Southern France and I should be with you." Instead, Colonel Yarborough gave me another assignment, which was to bring up the records and supplies by ship. He said, "I can't trust anybody else" with the mission, so I arrived a few days later by ship.

The 509th Parachute Infantry Combat Team spearheaded the airborne invasion of Southern France, jumping at St. Tropez and Le Muy. One whole stick of 17 paratroopers commanded by Captain Ralph Miller Jr. of Youngstown, Ohio, perished when they were mistakenly dropped into the Gulf of St. Tropez, and no bodies were ever recovered. Today there's a monument near the city cemetery with the names and home towns of all 17 troopers. I visited the monument with Captain Miller's family when I came back in 1946. It was a gut-wrenching experience. Captain Miller's father took me over to the courthouse to meet the switchboard operator, whose son was also in the 509th and was killed at Venafro.

When I arrived in Southern France, Colonel Yarborough had me and Lieutenant Harry H. Pritchett Jr. represent him at a dinner given by the local Free French of the Interior group. We had a strong aperitif before the dinner, red wine with the dinner and cognac after. When Harry and I left, we ran into a

FROM PARATROOPER TO PUBLIC DEFENDER

photographer who propped us up against a fountain and took our picture. My mother said she never saw me so relaxed.

We found a 1936 or '37 Cord sedan in a garage under a hotel, and the manager told us it belonged to Sidney Chaplin, the son of Charlie Chaplin. He had left the car when he got out in 1940 just before the Nazis came in. The Germans had taken the tires for rubber, so we put four GI tires on and ran around in it until December, when we left for Villers-Cotterets. It was a splendid car – a low-slung, cream colored sedan with the big flexible pipes going out of the hood. It had all red leather upholstery with a million dials on the dashboard and hand cranks to roll out the head and tail lights. It broke our hearts to leave it behind, but we did take the tires back.

We noticed that a local thief was stealing jerry cans of gas from the holders on the back of our jeeps. We set a trap by putting some cans of gas diluted with water and sugar on the back of a few jeeps. Some were stolen and we caught the crook when we saw his car stalled and sugar crystallizing out of the head gasket. It was satisfying to see the teed off look on his face.

In Southern France we had a company of six-wheeled M8 armored cars attached to the battalion. These cars had a powerful truck engine, and I wanted to drive one in the worst way. I took some of my men to the garage in Nice and gave the sergeant a song and dance about road testing. He reluctantly allowed us to have a car, and I had a great time whipping the car around the hairpin turns above Nice. On the way down we encountered a jeep coming up with, you guessed it, the commanding officer, who "owned" that particular armored vehicle. He was not a happy camper. We stopped, and the following exchange occurred.

"What the #$%@ are you doing with that ^&#%! armored car?"

"We're road testing it, Sir."

"Get that *#(@# car back to the)$^#@% garage and get it there now!!!"

We returned the car and luckily there were no repercussions, but we did have a great time.

Chapter 10: A Holiday Service

We were conducting operations in the mountains during the holidays of Rosh Hashana and Yom Kippur in 1944, and Lieutenant Sol Weber and I wanted to attend services. Weber had been the platoon sergeant of the signal platoon and had received a battlefield commission. We came down from the mountains and went into Nice, where we located a "storefront" synagogue whose congregation consisted of refugees keeping out of sight in Southern France.

The congregation was panicked when we walked in wearing full combat gear, steel helmets and armed to the teeth. We explained that we were just a couple of Jewish boys who wished to attend services. Immediately a prayer shawl was found for each of us, along with a yarmulke, or skull cap. We were seated up front, and each given a prayer book. We dropped our weapons on the floor and the service continued. Afterward we talked with the congregants who told us of what they had been through. They all had grim tales of Nazi persecution. When we left, they were praying for our safety, after all the horrors they had endured.

(When the 82nd Airborne Division was on occupation duty in Berlin in the summer of 1945, I met the sister of one of the FFI fighters when I went to the rest & recreation leave center in Nice. She had been there hiding from the Nazis and told me that the Italian military had been very active in protecting Jewish refugees from the Nazi secret police and the German military.)

In early December of 1944, we were withdrawn from Southern France and sent north to Villers Cotterets. On the way we saw the shattered remains of Nazi tanks and other vehicles that were destroyed by our aircraft. Because a unit there previously had blown the safe at the railroad station and stolen all the stamps, we were not well received. However, we received a shipment of oranges and arranged with the mayor of Villers Cotterets to give them out to the local children. Things went a lot better in town after that.

Our battalion C.O., Major Ed Tomasik of New Bedford, Mass., was ordered to go to Paris to bring our unit history and records to Brigadier General S.L.A. Marshall, the theater historian. It was a bitterly cold day and we drove there in an open jeep. A very pretty blonde WAC was typing away, and the office might as well have been in Washington or San Francisco. We mentioned the cold ride, and when Marshall's secretary asked why we didn't close in the jeep with plywood as others did, Tomasik told her that when we were shot at we had to "bail out" and hit the ditch as quickly as possible. Her eyes got as big as saucers and we realized she had never before met anyone who had been in combat.

By the way, Marshall managed to lose our records and we were never mentioned in his reports and history.

Tomasik and I also had to report to Brigadier General Jerry Higgins, assistant division commander of the 101st Airborne Division, at Mourmelon. He was a fine officer and told Tomasik that the next time he had to report there, to call him and a liaison plane would pick him up. There was no next time, as the division was almost immediately pulled out of Mourmelon and sent to Bastogne at the beginning of the Battle of the Bulge.

While at the 101st Airborne Division headquarters I ran into Captain Joseph Noonan, a classmate from Connecticut State. Joe wound up practicing law in Meriden and died while we were working on the 50th reunion of the Class of 1939.

Before we left Southern France, our C.O., Colonel Yarborough, was sent back to the States to go to command general staff college. He was on his way up in the ranks. The first thing he did when he arrived in the States was call my mother in Hartford and tell her I was all right. (When I got promoted to colonel, he sent me his own eagles to wear.)

Chapter 11: Maurice Rose: My Kind of General

After Southern France we were supposed to go to the Huertgen Forest, but we were sidetracked because the Battle of the Bulge broke out. We got orders by phone that there would be trucks to pick us up at 2 o'clock in the morning. We were to report to Major General Maurice Rose, commanding general of the 3rd Armored Division.

When I got to the Manhay crossroads, I had to report directly to Major General Rose. He was from Middletown, Connecticut, and I'm trying to get the town to name a road after him, Major General Maurice Rose Highway. He was a nice Jewish boy who'd been in World War I. He left the service and went back in, and had been commanding the 3rd Armored Division throughout the Belgian operation.

One of our younger officers made the mistake of telling him at a briefing that "Sir, our men haven't slept in 24 hours." Rose shot back, "Our men have not slept in 48 hours. You're fresh troops!" He was my kind of guy. He's the kind of leader I'm glad I was with. He was killed later on, when Eisenhower insisted that he had to push the Nazis back on all fronts. George S. Patton had the right idea: You surround them and squeeze them in. Rose ran up against a tank and reached to throw his gun down, and they shot him. He was a tremendous leader.

The 509th saw heavy combat during the Bulge at Manhay and Sadzot, Soy and Hotton. We were then attached to the 7th Armored Division and fought at Koenigswald. The 509th captured St. Vith and ended up at Trois Ponts with only seven officers and 43 men still standing.

Incidentally, when I was a student at Iowa State College, I met a girl who, when she found out I was going into the Army, told me her uncle was the 7th Armored Division commander and if I ever ran into him, I should give him her regards.

When we were attached to the 7th Armored Division, their commander, Major General Robert Hasbrouck, was inspecting the troops, asking things like where are you from and what did you do before the war. So I mentioned the girl's name and said she said to say hello. "Oh yes," he said, "that's my niece." And here I thought she was BS-ing me.

Also, I didn't know until several years after I graduated law school that one of my classmates, Howard Warner, was in the mortar platoon that was supporting us when we wiped out an SS regiment at Manhay.

FROM PARATROOPER TO PUBLIC DEFENDER

Chapter 12: Close Call at Sadzot

There are some memories that are always with you. There's nothing you can do about it. In Italy I spent some time as the graves registration officer. I'd sometimes go out on patrol in the morning, do my job as adjutant, then later at night I'd go forward with my jeep and my driver, pick up the bodies, and bring them back. You never knew what you were going to find. There was one foxhole with two bodies in it. I had two men with me, and I was trying to get the bodies out. I had two stretchers, and I was trying to get them on, and then I realized that I was up to my elbows in this man's guts. War is horrible. You know the memory is there, it fades away from time to time, but it's always there.[4]

---

[4] This duty led to Morton Katz receiving the Bronze Star Medal for heroic achievement in action. The citation reads: "During combat operations on the Anzio Beachhead from 31 January 1944 to 12 March 1944, Lieutenant Katz was responsible for the successful removal of fatal casualties from the forward positions of the Battalion near Carano. Companies were so depleted that no aid was available from them. It was necessary to bring up a GMC truck, proceed on foot over open field in bright moonlight, and remove the bodies from the thirty-foot gully. During this time the area was under shellfire and there was no cover. On 19 February 1944, Lieutenant Katz went to the position which had been under heavy enemy shelling all day and was then lighted by enemy flares. Under artillery and mortar fire, three trips were made over open ground. Following an all day barrage on 29 February 1944, Lieutenant Katz proceeded over an open field to recover three men in a dugout. Working in rain and total darkness, he evacuated the men over a stream at the bottom of a deep, slippery gully and across a half mile of open field crossed by ditches two to four feet in depth. His resourcefulness, perseverance and courage to carry out a most difficult job were responsible for prompt removal of bodies, and contributed to the high morale of the battalion."

FROM PARATROOPER TO PUBLIC DEFENDER

We would get replacements at the Anzio beachhead. After the first wave of the invasion, there was a small pier on one side where the replacements would get off the LSTs. You were not safe anywhere on the beachhead. And this replacement just gets off the LST and gets hit with a shot and gets killed. He got a stray shot, it just hit him.

We had to clean out, they had a bag or some other things, they didn't want to send home any lurid letters or a picture of some woman to a wife back in the States. So I opened this kid's barracks bag and there was a photograph in an imitation leather frame. It was a picture of a young girl. Now this kid obviously falsified his age, he wasn't anywhere near 18 years of age. That was bad enough. And I opened up the envelope, there was this picture of a very pretty young girl, maybe 14 or 15 years old, a high school romance. And I just thought how he would never see her again and she would never see him again. And I just fell apart.

But the closest I came to really losing it, there was a fellow who came to us, Harry Pritchett. He was in the West Point Class of '43, the one that was cut short because they needed company grade infantry officers, and we became very close. He was about as nuts as I was. He got the Silver Star in Italy. They were hounding us that they wanted a prisoner, so Harry grabs a rowboat from the river bank and all by himself goes over to the other bank and captures a sentry. As he's bringing the prisoner back, the guy got loose and they had a traditional knife fight, and Harry knifes this guy to death. Then he brings him into the headquarters, puts him on the floor, and says "There's your damn German."

When we were in Belgium, we were always short of people. After the battle at the Manhay crossroads, it was important for us to find out if there were still any SS in the woods south of Sadzot. So Harry and I went down this road. It was a cloudy, cold, dark day. We came to this area where one of our lousy light tanks had been shot up, and there was a young tanker just hanging out of the turret. And we saw some figures walking in the woods.

FROM PARATROOPER TO PUBLIC DEFENDER

The general test in those days was, if a guy had a long overcoat on he was probably a Kraut. So we ducked down. They were coming closer, and we were about 110 percent sure they were German. So we got down behind a log. Harry had a submachine gun with a full drum of 50 rounds, and I had a carbine, which had an extra magazine taped on the loaded gun. We were actually squeezing the triggers to cut these guys down. We were so close to firing I still can't believe it. And suddenly the clouds parted, the sky opened up, a shaft of sunlight came down and we could make out the uniforms. They were long overcoats but they had the red keystone insignia of the 28th Infantry Division, which was the federalized Pennsylvania Army National Guard. And we just crawled away. If we had fired, it would be easy to say they could have been German and there probably would have been no repercussions, but I would have known, and that's something that's hard to live with.

Some years later, at a veterans function, I was at the bar having a couple drinks with a guy, and we got to shooting the breeze. He said he was in the 28th Division, and that he was involved in the fight at Sadzot. He remembered going down the road, and seeing a burned out tank with a guy in the turret. We compared every possible factor. There was no question, I'm having a drink with a guy I damn near killed.

It was decided at SHAEF (Supreme Headquarters of the Allied Expeditionary Force) to disband all of the small, special units and reassign the personnel to the major Airborne units. In spite of orders that no enlisted personnel were to be reduced in rank as a result, many of our best non-commissioned officers were illegally reduced to private, mainly in the 82nd Airborne Division. This was in marked contrast to the fine treatment we received when we were attached to the 3rd Armored Division. On Christmas Day in 1944 we were in combat in the Manhay-Erezee area and there were no rations. We were also short on supplies. Around noon, a convoy of halftracks from Lieutenant Colonel Richardson's 33rd Armored Infantry came down the highway to our positions, delivering hot, roast stuffed turkey in insulated marmite cans.

While we were conducting operations in the Ardennes, we were assigned to XVIII Airborne Corps under the command of Lieutenant General Matthew B. Ridgway, who had commanded the 82nd Airborne Division. We were in the Soy-Hotton area. Most of the Corps staff had come up from the 82nd Airborne Division and continued its discrimination against the 509th. Colonel Schellhammer, the Corps G-1, denied our C.O., Major Ed Tomasik, his well-earned promotion to lieutenant colonel. (In October of 1944, while we were in Southern France, Lieutenant Colonel Yarborough was ordered back to the States. Major Tomasik assumed command and had more command time in combat than was required for promotion to lieutenant colonel). Schellhammer made sure Tomasik never received his promotion – in spite of which Tomasik remained on active duty after the war and retired as a full O-6 colonel.

During these operations I took a young trooper to XVIII Airborne Corps headquarters to receive the Silver Star from General Ridgway. Some pompous staff officer would not allow me to come into General Ridgway's office for the ceremony. Years later, at a convention of the 82nd Airborne Division, I told Ridgway the story. He apologized to me and told me that I had every right to be there and the staff officer was dead wrong in barring me from the ceremony.

I was one of a number of our officers, non-coms and men transferred to the 82nd Airborne Division. Most went to the 505th Parachute Infantry, one of the regiments. Most of the men were received very badly and treated very poorly. Lieutenant Colonel Ireland, Division G-1, had lied to me about Colonel Bill Ekman's having asked for me. However, Ekman assigned me as Assistant S-2, intelligence officer, and since the assigned S-2 was always off on some choice deal, such as running a displaced persons camp or going to school in Paris, I was in fact working the S-2 until the end of the war.

With the 505th I went to the Rhine River, where we captured the oil plant at Weseling before it could open, and ran patrols across the river. I had occasion to test fire the new 75mm recoilless rifles across the Rhine. Sergeant Teague dropped a round through the vision slit of a pillbox on the third shot. The 75mm recoilless was a remarkable weapon and very accurate in the hands of Sergeant Teague.

I had occasion to conduct a homicide investigation while I was with the 505th. We fished a dead Gestapo agent out of the river one morning after a car ran our roadblock. There had been some shooting along the river the night before. After an investigation with one of my best interrogators, involving an adjacent French unit, German prostitutes, French forced laborers and some delicate inquiries of the French, we concluded it was a revenge killing of the agent who had learned of the laborers being with the prostitutes and turning them in to the authorities. We recommended that the French keep their activities in their own sector and that was the end of it.

Chapter 13: The Concentration Camp

On the way to the Elbe River we picked up an escaped German prisoner named Brahms, no relation to the composer. Since he could speak Russian, I commandeered him as our German-Russian interpreter. We nearly got shot by panicky green troops of the 86th Infantry Division as we moved to the Elbe.

The Division crossed the Elbe at Bleckede on the morning of 30 April 1945. I was in the lead landing boat with the commanding officer of the 505th Parachute Infantry, Colonel Ekman, under intense artillery fire. When we hit the other bank, Major General James Gavin, commanding our 82nd Airborne Division, was there to meet us. He was wearing his beat-up old jump suit, carrying his own M-1 rifle. As always, he would go in first, never sending anyone where he would not go first.

In addition to heavy artillery fire, the Germans had mined the far river bank with mines containing 75 pounds of explosive that could be detonated three different ways. One of our trucks set off a mine with the pressure trip, sending the GMC 2 ½ ton, six wheel truck into the air. The driver was blown out of the truck and the truck came down right beside him, just missing his head. The driver survived.

We made the river crossing okay. My sergeant got himself a box of 200 Dutch cigars, and in one of the houses we found a case of 24 bottles of Mount Vernon Square rye whisky. The Germans had hidden so much booze there that the British couldn't drink it all, and they could drink anything.

At about this time the German 21st Army surrendered to our regiment.

We chased the enemy through the Bleckede, Alt Jabel, Ludwigslust and Vielank area, liberating the Wobbelin concentration camp at Ludwigslust.

FROM PARATROOPER TO PUBLIC DEFENDER

At the concentration camp I went into a warehouse, and there were thousands of pairs of wooden clogs that had been worn by the inmates and workers who starved to death.

My S-2 section captured the Nazi colonel commanding the camp. While I was tearing the office apart, looking for lists of people, names and records, the commandant's wife got all bent out of shape. So I told my interpreter, you tell that Nazi pig to either shut her god damn mouth or I'm going to cut her throat.

General Gavin was so outraged by the Wobbelin camp that he made the local populace carry the bodies into Ludwigslust and bury them in the town square. And everywhere we went, it was the same: "We didn't know what was going on." In Ludwigslust we found a strap that they were using to beat the laborers. Like hell they didn't know. They were making money out of it, too.

Among the things I found in the office was a book about the 1936 Olympics that included Ivan Fuqua's triumph in track and field. Ivan had become track coach at the University of Connecticut, and I sent him the book.

There was no problem with the enemy troops, as their concern was to get to us in order to avoid falling into the hands of the Soviets. While we were leapfrogging with the Regimental Headquarters en route to meet at the next rendezvous point, my convoy of some four jeeps of the S-2 section stopped at a farmhouse to determine if all was clear. We pulled into the farmyard to check the house. It was empty, and on the stove was a large pot of boiling water. On the counter was a large brownstone crock filled with fresh eggs. My unit, not having seen fresh eggs for a while, looked at me with an unspoken question. I gave an OK nod and one of the men with a culinary skill started on the eggs. We had boiled eggs, fried eggs, scrambled eggs, and I thought it would be in order to clean up. I took off my steel "pot," got some hot water, stripped to the waist, and took a "helmet bath."

Then I lathered up to take a shave. Standing there, my inverted helmet on my jeep, face full of lather, stripped to the waist, I saw another convoy of jeeps roar into the yard. The lead vehicle sported a red plate with a silver star the size of a pyramidal tent. It was Brigadier General Ira P. Swift, Assistant Division Commander. He jumped out and sounded off: "Who's in charge here!"

I responded, "I am."

"And you are?"

Slightly unnerved, I answered: "First Lieutenant Katz, S-2, 505th Parachute Infantry."

"And what's going on here?"

"We're linking up with Colonel Ekman at the next checkpoint," I said, looking at my watch.

Of course, Swift knew what was going on – we were goofing off. He had a suspicious grin and said "Carry on," and his convoy took off from the farmyard. We did manage to finish all the eggs.

That wasn't the only time I bent the rules. The base section commander in Paris was a sonofabitch named Major General Evans. He would gig people for no good reason. And Major Iron Mike O'Daniel was sending his combat front line people back to Naples from the Anzio beachhead to give them a couple days R&R, so Evans got the MPs to pick these men up getting off the LST, tear up their passes and lock them up for the weekend. O'Daniel gets wind of this. He didn't go through channels. He went right up to General Mark Clark. I don't know exactly what Clark said to Evans but it was something to the effect, he just picked the phone up with O'Daniel in the room and said something to the effect of "Knock it off."

So we had come back to that area to the redeployment camp and we were sending men to the redeployment camp called Oklahoma City, which was a mud hole, and we'd give the guys some time in Paris. They'd earned it. So Evans had these roving patrols, and they'd pick a guy up and court martial him if his hat was on sloppy or a button was unbuttoned. And it was all the same thing: Guilty. Reduction in rank to private.

So we're in the office. By that time I was personnel officer, and it was a cold, crappy day, and the fire was dying out. We get this package from Seine Bay Section, and we open it up. It's court martial records for our old time sergeants. So we sat there, and we looked at one another and nodded, and we started to throw the court martial records in the fire. They burned until 2 in the morning. And we forgot about it. Until we got to Le Havre and we get a letter, "You have not replied by endorsement to certain court martial records." So I wrote back through channels, I said, "No record this headquarters of any such records." By the time they sent another letter out we were already halfway home.

On 3 May 1945 the German XXI Army surrendered to the 82nd Airborne Division at Ludwigslust. It was very satisfying to have the job of taking one of the German generals, along with some of his staff, to the POW compound. I crowded them into my jeep and dropped them off at the prisoner of war area.

Chapter 14: Descendent of Aaron

After returning to Sissonne, France, we were prepared for occupation duty in Berlin. We entered Berlin early in the summer and set up headquarters in the Schlachtensee area. I was transferred to serve as Regimental Personnel Officer and had the opportunity to spend a week in the Southern France R&R area. I spent a week at a luxury hotel (the California Hotel in Cannes). It was an interesting trip back to Berlin, as the pilot took me forward and I was in the co-pilot's seat all the way.

I was able to attend service for the High Holy Days of Rosh Hashanah and Yom Kippur. The military chaplain of the Berlin district was a rabbi, and he reopened and re-consecrated the principal synagogue in Berlin. This had been closed and desecrated when the Nazis came to power. The chaplain found out I was a Kohane, a direct descendant of Aaron, the brother of Moses, designating me as a High Priest of Israel. This entitled me to give the first blessing at the reading of the Torah, the sacred scroll.

At the service, over half the congregation was made up of Soviet soldiers, with the soft garrison cap, the baggy blouse, and the boots. They carried worn prayer books, long hidden from the Soviet authorities. It was an indescribable feeling to be on the pulpit, giving the first blessing at the first service since the Nazis had closed the synagogue. I felt like Judah Maccabee after he had driven the Syrians and Greeks from the land of Israel.

I stayed in the Army Reserve after coming home with the 82nd Airborne Division. (My regiment, the 505th Parachute Infantry, led the Victory Parade up Fifth Avenue in New York City in January of 1946.) I went to the University of Connecticut Law School on the GI Bill, and served 17 years in the 411th Civil Affairs Company, West Hartford, the last eight years as commanding officer. When I was promoted to colonel,

FROM PARATROOPER TO PUBLIC DEFENDER

Lieutenant General Yarborough had me assigned to the Office of the Assistant Chief of Staff, Intelligence G-2 at the Pentagon, where I worked with the Defense Intelligence Agency.

In 1972 I was retired after 34 years of service. The Office of the Assistant Chief of Staff for Intelligence awarded me the Legion of Merit and I had received the Bronze Star Medal (V) with Oakleaf Cluster; Army Commendation Medal; European-African-Middle Eastern Service Medal, Medal of French Liberation, and Reserve Service Medal. With the 509th I was awarded the Presidential Unit Citation with two Oakleaf Clusters for actions at Anzio and the Ardennes and with the 505th for action in Germany. I earned the Combat Infantry Badge and Parachute Qualification Badge.

Campaigns in which I participated as a member of the 509th and the 505th were:

Algeria-French Morocco
Tunisia
Naples-Foggia
Rome-Arno
Anzio
Southern France
Rhineland
Ardennes
Central Europe

Chapter 15: Coming Home

When I came back, I didn't know what I was doing. I took a trip around the country. One thing I had to do is I made a deal with Captain Ralph Miller that if one of us didn't make it back, the survivor would go and see the family, so I did. He didn't make it back. They went into Southern France and they came in over St. Tropez, and they hadn't issued the parachute you could take off quickly, pull a safety clip out, push a button, the whole thing falls off. So if this webbing gets wet, it gets tight, you can't get out of it. So he was killed in Southern France.

That was tough. I didn't tell them exactly what happened, that some stupid brass hat couldn't issue the right equipment. They kept me there for the weekend. I went to church with them. As I was leaving, they said there was someone they would like me to meet at the courthouse. It turned out that this lady was a switchboard operator, and I didn't know her son, you can't know everybody in the outfit. Her son was in the outfit and he was killed in Onofro.

Then I went back to Iowa. I ran into my major professor. He said, "You have to come back to get your Ph. D." So I came back, and just for the hell of it, I put in for a minor in chemical engineering and I did better than I had done before. I did so good I got a teaching fellowship. And after a while I realized I hated the damn research, but I liked teaching, because I was working with people. So I went ovr to the VA, and they had very good counselors, and they gave me examinations. My counselor said, "My advice to you is get the hell out of here. You have no interest whatsoever and no aptitude for science."

I resigned my fellowship. I went to law school at the University of Connecticut and I graduated law school with honors. I never made a million dollars, but it was the place I should be.

When I started out, I got a lucky break in timing. I wanted to get in a Reserve unit so I could get paid, and I went to the 76th Division, which was getting a new tank company. So I went to the chief of staff, and he said "If you go to the armor school, they'll give you the command of a company."

So I went to the armor school, and while I was there, the Korean War broke out.

While I was at Fort Knox, they gave single officers not only quarters, but a quarters allowance on top of that, and I bought my first car. I was 31 years old, an officer in the Army, and it was the first chance I had to buy a car. I bought a Chevy Impala. The reason I got it, this guy had bought the car, put a deposit down, and he was ordered to active duty. Hopefully they gave him his money back. It was the new imitation hardtop, four cylinder, great little car. I took it to Fort Benning the next year when I went for the advance course in the infantry school. Then on the way back to Iowa State, I got two weeks of active duty.

Then I got into a unit, because our instructor had said, "You'd better get into a unit or you may find yourself in Korea." And it worked out great, because several high ranks were available. Then one of the majors was transferred to somewhere in the Midwest, and then somebody else dropped out.

I had an interesting experience. I wasn't there, but they were talking about promotions, and they were starting to clamp down. Unless you had certain advanced courses, you didn't get promoted. And the commander, a Lieutenant Colonel Vecchiola, they were talking about the promotion status and someone said, "Captain Katz has been to the advance course at the infantry school. He could be promoted."

And the executive officer said, "Oh, but Captain Katz is Jewish."

And Vecchiola said, "In that case we'll promote him right away."

So, this is part of my life. I'm going to add a few things which I think are worthwhile. I had been up for promotion eight or nine times and was sent to the wrong headquarters or the records were lost, there was a plane crash, all sorts of things, and you had a choice: whether you want to stay in the Reserves or not. Officers were not discharged. Rather, they were released from extended active duty.

I was within a hairsbreadth of saying "the hell with it." But I found out that if you had an overall rating above a certain figure, you would automatically get a one-jump promotion. So I said hey, why not? I signed and was promoted to captain. I wound up having command of a reserve unit, and that was it.

I got the promotion to captain, and it worked out great. I retired out of the Pentagon. My first son-in-law is involved with government computers, I don't know if he builds or repairs them. He was down at the agency a couple of years ago for a ceremony and he got me a crystal mug and a hat. And he said, "I'm buying this for my father-in-law, Colonel Morton Katz." And a man in the store said, "I know that name." And this guy was one of my analysts in the 1960s.

But you've got to be tough to stick it out. You go to the annual training, and I don't care what you are, everything is making you feel like crap. One time a regular sergeant said "Where's my work party?" and I let him have it.

I met my wife in 1961. I wanted to go to John Dempsey's inaugural ball as governor of Connecticut. I had just gotten my new Army dress blues, and I'd just been dumped by some girl, thank God. So the Gerson brothers, whom my father and I had known for years, fixed me up with a date a couple of days before the ball. At the last minute, though, she had to go back to Minnesota to see her mother or something. Then one of my clients set me up with a pharmacist who worked in a big pharmacy. I called her and we went to the ball and had a wonderful time. We started off slowly, and then I woke up one morning and a voice came down from Mount Sinai, "Morton

Katz, you bloody damn jackass, this is the girl! Don't let her go!" That's all it took.

When I started out as a lawyer, it was impossible to get an office. My father would ask some lawyer he knew and they would say "Have Mort drop over to my office." Of course all the lawyer would tell me was that there's no place for you in this office. So I started out in Uncle Bill Bernstein's office. He taught me a lot about title work. We did a lot of closings. He did a lot of work for big developers.

There was a development known as Green Acres. I did most of the title work on the big tracts that they broke up into individual lots to sell. And I was able to do a lot of work for them.

Of course I was an unpaid intern, I would go to closings and I was paid nickels and dimes. Bernstein didn't want me to contact or talk with his clients. And it was a handicap because he did have one situation where I did the title, and I ran across in the books what you call a caveat. Now the caveat was on the record, but it wasn't an encumbrance because it didn't affect the transfer of the property. All it said was that sometime in the distant future if this happens and so forth there may be a sewer coming through here. It was just a warning and had nothing to do with the title. And the other lawyer got all pissed off and said, "I can't let my client buy this." If I had been there with Bernstein, I could have explained. I had the book there, "Standards of Title."

So eventually he got on my nerves, on top of which, he wanted me to pay rent, so I should be a subtenant.

Around that time, Abe Ribicoff became governor of Connecticut. My father was doing a lot of title work for John Bailey, and a fellow named Joe Fauliso in Bailey's office got an appointment as a city court judge. That meant that other lawyers in Bailey's office could not go into city court because they were in the office of Fauliso.

So Fauliso opened his own office, and I got a call and I talked to Joe and explained that yes, I did title work and I'd be happy to come in with you. And I explained, very carefully, I said "Now, I

FROM PARATROOPER TO PUBLIC DEFENDER

want you to know, I'm not just a veteran, I'm in the Army Reserve and it's important to me because the Army Reserve is my first step to retirement." And he was always rushing, rush here, rush there, and he never quite understood what the Army thing was all about. And that was involving one night a week at the South Quaker Lane Reserve Center and two weeks a year at whatever post they sent us to for field training. And we also were expected to go to various service schools to get promoted. And if you didn't get promoted in a certain period of time, you were out.

(Fauliso went on to become a state senator and eventually served as president pro tem of the Senate. He became lieutenant governor upon the resignation of his close friend, Governor Ella Grasso, who was terminally ill.)

We got some work from the Society for Savings to do title work at closings. We had them in our offices, and then we had some work at an office in New Britain. They weren't a bank, but they were like a bank, and they were cutting into our business, and we were not really making any money.

Eventually Ella Grasso became the governor of Connecticut, and I wanted to be on the governor's military staff. And I had an angle. I said to Joe, "You have Ella Grasso's ear. All I want, it's not a money job, and I'd like to be on the staff." So I got the position, and it was a lot of fun. I had my new Army dress blues and so forth.

I didn't know this until a long time later, Ella Grasso took a liking to me. She didn't want to be pushy. We had several guys because that's a pretty good state job, being on the staff. And I probably could have been, if I had wanted to and had known about this, I probably could have been a judge.

Sometime around 1997 I saw an advertisement in a law journal that the state was looking for public defenders. The position was assistant public defender. You got $350 a case. But it was an experience. And I worked with a lot of regular public defenders, and they were competent and very helpful. And I started doing very well in the courts.

FROM PARATROOPER TO PUBLIC DEFENDER

Then I was appointed as a magistrate. I had a lot of fun doing it. I had a guy who came from the Caribbean, he kept calling me My Lord. And I signed up for statewide legal services. You get absolutely pro bono. And I was doing a lot of work in that department for people who had been unjustly fired and then denied unemployment compensation. I would do the appeals for them, and I was very successful. I only lost two cases. One was a guy who was told by his employer, "You don't have enough time here for a vacation, and you're not gonna go on vacation." So he said the hell with it and went on vacation. I took that case and it was just a waste of time.

I got an award as a special public defender when I was ninetysomething, and then I got another award for overall or all-time public service in the Supreme Court, and the chief justice made a speech, then he comes down off the bench and he's holding a box behind him, so he eventually opens the box and there's a straw hat. I make a big thing about it. I was born on May 15th, which is Straw Hat Day. I wear the straw hat starting every May 15th.

FROM PARATROOPER TO PUBLIC DEFENDER

History of the 509th Parachute Infantry Battalion

By MORTON N. KATZ

(This unit history was written shortly after the war)

Organized as the original 504th Parachute Battalion (See: The parachute battalion photo album published by The Army & Navy Publishing Co., Inc., in 1942), the 2nd Battalion, 503rd Parachute Infantry left the United States on 4 June 1942 under Lieutenant Colonel Edson D. Raff, Jr. and landed in the United Kingdom at Gouroch, Scotland, on 10 June 1942. It was the first American airborne unit to go overseas. The Battalion was stationed at Chilton Foliat, estate of Lady Ward, in Hungerford, Berkshire. The unit trained with the First British Airborne Division under (then) Major General Sir Frederick A.W. Browning. The members were made honorary members of the Division and given the honor of wearing the famous "Red Devil" beret of the British Airborne.

After training in England (See: Time Magazine, Oct. 12, 1942, p. 67, and The New York Times Magazine, Jan. 3, 1943, p. 4), plans were made for the North African invasion. On the night of 7 November 1942 the Battalion took off from Land's End, England, the first U.S. parachute unit to enter combat, bound for Tafaraoui Airport in Oran, Algeria. The unit arrived 8 November after flying 1,600 miles, the longest airborne invasion in history (See: The American Magazine, March 1943, p. 126). Three planes were forced down in Spanish Morocco and all personnel interned for three months. Some were forced down in the Sebkra d'Oran, a salt sandy waste, by enemy fighter planes which strafed the helpless ships (See: Look Magazine, July 13, 1943, p. 52).

FROM PARATROOPER TO PUBLIC DEFENDER

Lieutenant Dave Kunkle was killed in his plane, the first parachute officer to die. Among other casualties was Private John C. Mackall of Company E, in whose memory is named Camp Mackall at Hoffman, North Carolina, the Army's largest airborne training center. Captain (later Major) William J. Moir later received the Distinguished Service Cross for his work as medical officer. He is both the first parachute officer and first parachute medic to be decorated (See: Look Magazine, as above).

After defending Tafaraoui Airport against the French Foreign Legion coming from Sidi Bel Abbes, the group reorganized and went to Maison Blanche Airport near Algiers. From here the troops took off on 15 November 1942, crossing the Atlas Mountains towards Tebessa on the Tunisian border, jumping at Youks-les-Bains near Thelepte Airport. This airport became the base for Colonel Phil Cochran, famous as Milt Caniff's "Flip" Corkin. The troopers and members of the Third (French) Zouave Regiment formed a combined defense in the area and Colonel Geuges presented the regimental insignia of the Zouaves to the Battalion. Confirmed by AFHQ (Allied Force Headquarters), this "award" is worn today by those troopers.

The Battalion was the first American unit in Tunisia and first to contact Rommel's Afrika Korps, first in Gafsa, fought at Sbeitla, Feriana, Kasserine Pass, and in the first battle of Faid Pass, which was taken by a combined parachutist, infantry, tirailleur and TD (tank destroyer) team.

The third combat jump was led by Lieutenant Dan A. DeLeo, of Chicago, when he took two planes with some 32 men to El Djem, Tunisia to blow the bridge. Although he had only six weeks of stateside troop experience, his men were replacements untrained as a unit, and the captain who was to command the mission was able to back out at the last minute, Lieutenant DeLeo partially accomplished his mission (See: Look Magazine, March 9, 1943, p. 42). He was dropped on the wrong side of the tracks, too close to the town at the wrong end of the bridge, from planes flying in the wrong direction, with French guides who did not know the country. Although DeLeo and his men were betrayed by Arabs in the pay of the Germans, he and his men blew up an armored train, destroyed much trackage and caused havoc and confusion among the enemy.

Promoted to full Colonel, Raff was relieved to go to the States (See: "We Jumped to Fight," by Edson D. Raff, Jr.). The major portion of the Battalion, under newly promoted Lieutenant Colonel Doyle R. Yardley of Raymondville, Texas, had gone from Maison Carres near Algiers to Boufarik for further training. In the U.S., the 503rd Parachute Infantry Regiment had acquired a new 2nd Battalion from the 502nd, and to avoid confusion the unit in North Africa was redesignated the 2nd Battalion, 509th Parachute Infantry.

Assigned to the newly formed 5th Army at the request of General Mark E. Clark, the outfit moved to Oujda, French Morocco, and built Camp Kunkle, named in memory of Lieutenant Dave Kunkle. About this time, 29 April 1943, the 82nd Airborne Division left the Zone of the Interior, arriving in Casablanca on 10 May 1943, and coming to Oujda, *after* the Tunisian campaign closed, on 12 May 1943. Prior to the Sicilian campaign, the group moved to Kairouan, Tunisia with the Division and remained in 7th Army reserve for the campaign, along with the 325th Glider Infantry.

On 9 September 1943, the Parachute Scout Company under the late Captain Charles C.W. Howland of Tallapoosa, Georgia left Bizerte as part of a joint Army-Navy task force for the amphibious operation in Naples Harbor (this was the operation that writer Quentin Reynolds wrongly credited to Commander Douglas Fairbanks, Jr. and John Steinbeck in Colliers Magazine for 23 October 1943.) The troopers captured the islands of Ventotene, Ischia, Procida, Capri and Ponza, missing the Italian Fascist dictator Benito Mussolini by seven hours on the last-named island. They captured the radar station and hundreds of German troops without losing a man, under the very noses of the enemy. Captain Howland received the Legion of Merit, and Sergeant Amarante Garcia the Silver Star with two other men.

From Comiso, Sicily, the Battalion took off the night of 14-15 September 1943, for its fourth combat jump. This jump, at Avellino, Italy was a desperate mission to cut German supply and communications lines and relieve pressure on the Salerno beachhead. Although the men were widely scattered, the mission was successful despite the capture of Lieutenant Colonel Yardley, Lieutenant Jack Pogue and about 119 men, the Germans being completely disorganized by what they thought was a larger unit.

After reorganizing in the Piscinola district in Naples, the unit, now commanded by Lieutenant Colonel William P. Yarborough, Jr., of Staunton, Virginia went to Macchia and then to Venafro, across the Volturno River. This operation lasted from 9 November 1943 to 14 December 1943 until relieved by the 45th Infantry Division. On 11 November, the unit captured Mount Corno in Venafro, working with the Rangers and the 45th Infantry Division. Mount Croce was held against many enemy attacks. (See: Coronet Magazine, June 1944, p. 3.) During this period the Battalion was redesignated the 509th Parachute Infantry Battalion.

Following intensive training and amphibious practice at Baia Bay in the Pozzuoli area of Naples, the Battalion took part in the D-Day landing on the Anzio-Nettuno beachhead at H plus 2 on 22 January 1944. The unit landed with the ill-fated Ranger force and later worked with the 3rd Infantry Division. On the beachhead the Battalion suffered some of its heaviest casualties. Here Staff Sergeant (now Master Sergeant) Paul B. Huff, of Cleveland, Tennessee, then with Company A, became the first parachutist to receive the Congressional Medal of Honor (See: The Infantry Journal, August 1944, p. 53.) (The dead Kraut on Page 51 of Life Magazine, Feb. 21, 1944, was killed by one of our B.A.R. men on D-Day. If you see this photo, he is on the curb, not the center line, and the vehicle in the background is an Italian prime mover for 155-millimeter artillery, not a command car.)

On 29 February 1944, the Battalion stopped a desperate drive by four battalions of the German 1028th Infantry Regiment in the Carano sector near Garibaldi's Tomb, designed to split the 45th Infantry Division on the left from the 3rd Infantry Division on the right, drive to the water and divide the beachhead. For stopping this drive in spite of the nearly complete loss of Company B, the Battalion became the first U.S. parachute unit to win the War Department (Presidential) Unit Citation: the troopers were the first to wear the Distinguished Unit Badge. (See: The Infantry Journal, July 1944, p. 40.)

Moving to Lido di Roma just after the fall of Rome, the Battalion became the nucleus of the so-called First Airborne Task Force, and the only combat-experienced unit in it, aside from the First Special Service Force. On 15 August 1944, the 509th made its fifth combat jump, landing at Le Muy, Southern France to spearhead the 7th Army invasion. Aided by the 463rd Parachute Field Artillery Battalion whose guns were firing in 20 minutes, the troopers rapidly captured the town. Two companies, Company B and Company C, landed at St. Tropez, and took that town. Linking up, the unit went east to liberate Cannes, Juan-les-Pins, Antibes and Nice, some of the troops (unofficially) entering neutral Monaco. As the first Americans to enter these towns, they received an enthusiastic welcome from the FFI (Free French of the Interior) and the populace.

Moving north, the 509th went to La Courbaisse to work with the FFI, then to Lantosque and the ski resort of Peira Cava near the northern Italian border. There were considerable mines, and heavy fighting in the Fort Milles Fourches area. On 23 November 1944, the 509th was withdrawn from the lines to La Gaude, west of Nice, across the Var River. Major General Robert T. Frederick presented decorations, awarding the unit its streamer as a Combat Infantry Battalion, and one for its Unit Citation. While in the Maritime Alps area, the Battalion was awarded the French Croix de Guerre with Silver Star (French Decision 246, 15 July 1946) for action on D-Day, 15 August 1944, at Muy en Provence.

On 8 December 1944, the unit left Nice by train and motor, arriving at Villers-Cotterets on 11 December. It was attached to the 101st Airborne Division, then stationed in Mourmelon. The 101st was very cooperative, having the barracks prepared, hot food ready. Brigadier General Gerald J. Higgins placed a Piper Cub at the disposal of Major Edmund J. Tomasik of New Bedford, Massachusetts, who replaced Lieutenant Colonel

Yarborough as commander when the latter went to Command & General Staff College in October.

When Field Marshal Gerd von Runstedt and Sepp Dietrich made the Ardennes breakthrough, the Battalion left on 22 December 1944 for Werbomont, Belgium. On arrival at Manhay, however, the group was attached to the 3rd Armored Division, as Major General Maurice Rose's only reserve. The troopers were to hold the Manhay-Grandmenil-Erezée supply line at all costs. On 24 December 1944. Company B and a platoon of Company A cleared the Soy-Hotton road, rescuing elements of 3rd Armored Headquarters that had been cut off. Company A and Company C sustained heavy losses at the road junction south of Manhay, which was lost at the "high water mark" of the offensive. The unit also had to help out the inexperienced 75th Infantry Division, which made such a poor showing in Belgium. In two days of bloody fighting at Sadzot, the troopers thoroughly defeated the First and Second Battalions of the 12th SS Regiment of the 25th SS Panzergrenadier Division.

For its fighting during the period 22-30 December, the Battalion received its second War Department (so-called Presidential) Unit Citation, this one from XVIII Corps (Airborne). 509th men hung the Oakleaf Cluster on the Distinguished Unit Badge; men of Company C putting on their second cluster. Following a brief rest and training with the 9th Armored Division in Kin and Lorce, Belgium, the Battalion was attached to the 7th Armored Division to clear the way for the drive south to St. Vith.

In bitter fighting in the snow on 20 January 1945, costing the lives of the famous Captain Charles C.W. Howland and Captain Leslie Winship – a former soldier of fortune who won the Medaille Militaire with the Foreign Legion – and resulting in another capture of the fabulous medical officer, Captain (now Lieutenant Colonel, USAF) Carlos C. Alden, Jr., of Buffalo, New York, the vital road junction of Born was captured unaided. In the next few days, the Battalion captured Hunningen and cleared the woods north of St. Vith. The 7th Armored then rolled through St. Vith unopposed.

Pushing south, the 509th took the high ground covering the main route south from St. Vith and held it until 29 January 1945, when seven officers and 48 men came down the hill to be relieved. All others were dead or hospitalized. Men and officers continued to come in to the new headquarters at Trois Ponts as they were released from hospitals. In February the blow fell – due to changes in tables of organization, and the consolidation of units for the final push on Germany, no place existed for separate parachute infantry battalions. The 509th was to be disbanded. Officers and men were to be transferred to the 82nd Airborne Division and the 13th Airborne Division, both units which could use the outstanding, combat-experienced veterans of the 509th. The Battalion was officially disbanded by War Department orders on 1 March 1945. One of the dark notes was the deliberate violation by the 82nd Airborne Division of direct orders prohibiting reduction of enlisted men as a result of the reorganization. Many outstanding NCOs were "busted" without cause.

Men of the 509th were among the first to be considered for rotation and redeployment in their divisions, due to their length of service and many decorations. They were outstanding as reinforcements. (See: The Chicago Tribune, 1 Feb. 1945.)

In its overseas history, the unit earned eight battle honors for Algeria-French Morocco, Tunisia, Naples-Foggia, Anzio, Rome-Arno, Southern France, Rhineland and Ardennes. Invasion arrowheads were included in the first four and the sixth. The 509th was a Combat Infantry Battalion, won the Distinguished Unit Badge and Oakleaf Cluster (two clusters for Company C), was awarded the French Croix de Guerre with Silver Star, given two Army and two Corps commendations and the regimental insignia of the 3rd (French) Zouave Regiment, and given honorary membership in the 1st British Airborne Division.

Individuals earned the Congressional Medal of Honor (first to be given an American parachutist), 10 Distinguished Service Crosses, 62 Silver Star Medals and two Oakleaf Clusters, 5 Legion of Merit awards, 38 Bronze Star Medals and two Oakleaf

FROM PARATROOPER TO PUBLIC DEFENDER

Clusters, 3 Soldier's Medals, and 6 Croix de Guerre with Silver Star decorations.

Its unit records include being the first parachute or airborne outfit overseas and in combat, making the longest airborne invasion in history, most number of combat parachute jumps in the European-African-Middle Eastern Theater; first into Tunisia, first to fight alongside and be commended by the French; first to fight the Afrika Korps; first into Southern France; first to jump with a war correspondent. While in England, members of Hq and Hq Company made the lowest altitude mass parachute jump of all time, 143 feet. It was the *only* parachute (airborne) unit to fight in North Africa.

Letter to Eileen

After sitting for a video interview with the Central Connecticut State University Veterans History Project, Morton wrote the following letter to Eileen Hurst, the program's director:

25 December 2006
Merry Christmas

Eileen: Thanks for the parking permit.

I corrected the spelling errors on the video log. In order to give you a more accurate presentation, I have set up a fully chronological presentation of the war experience, starting with my being commissioned and going through to my retirement.

Basic ROTC at Connecticut State College (now University of Connecticut) was compulsory when I started in 1935. I could not take advanced ROTC due to afternoon science labs, so I enrolled in CMTC (Citizens' Military Training Camps) and took the "White" and "Blue" courses at Fort Devens, MA and was commissioned 2LT Infantry (Organized Reserve) 12 June 1940.

While doing graduate study at (then) Iowa State College, Pearl Harbor was attacked 7 December 41 and I was ordered to EAD (Extended Active Duty) within a few days and sent to Fort Des Moines for a physical. Wrote my thesis and took my orals and went home to Hartford, ditched my "civvies," went into uniform and then to Fort H.G. Wright at Fishers Island for final physical April 1942.

Via Southern Railroad to head for Fort Benning, GA to take the Rifle & Heavy Weapons Company Commanders Course at the Infantry School. First shock was the segregation of the train at Washington, D.C. and the segregation signs in the Atlanta, GA railroad station. Some clerk tried to put three hundred fifty officers in a two hundred slot class, so one hundred fifty of us

FROM PARATROOPER TO PUBLIC DEFENDER

went to the Harmony Church area of the post (this was actually the OCS training area and the cadre/instructors, mainly recent OCS grads, had a great time working us over).

The course was excellent and very worthwhile (my lack of knowledge was extensive and I would have had a bad time without this instruction). During this time a MAJ Shinberger and 1LT Julian Cook conducted a recruiting session for The Parachute School. At the end of the evening Shinberger asked us all to sign an "attendance roster." Of course, all who did found that we had "volunteered" for the Jump Course. The Infantry School course graduated in early July 1942 and I went to The Parachute School. On graduating 15 August 1942 I was sent to the 502nd Parachute Infantry and assigned to Company "I", 3rd Battalion (the Adjutant was 1LT Raymond Bottomly whom I encountered later in 1963 when he was Chief oif Staff of XIII Corps at Fort Devins. He was at our wedding in November 1964 and let us use half of his permanent quarters at Annual Field Training the following year.

The Regiment was at the Alabama Training Area of Benning for some six weeks and then assigned to Fort Bragg, NC to form the 101st Airborne Division. I had occasion to meet MG William C. Lee, the "Father of the Airborne". The Regiment was at Bragg about six days and I was ordered to have all Second Lieutenants report to Regimental Headquarters. Twelve of us and one hundred sixty basic Privates were sent as a replacement package via the "Queen Elizabeth" to England. We arrived at Scotland and after passing through Litchfield Barracks and then Tidworth Barracks we ended up at Chilton Foliat, Hungerford, Berkshire, around the first of October 1942 with the 2nd Battalion, 503rd Parachute Infantry, commanded by (then) LTC Edson D. Raff, Jr.

Raff advised us that we were not supposed to be there, but were to have joined him later in the "combat zone." We did not know the Battalion was staging for the North Africa invasion (Operation "Torch"). The unit went to the staging area and took off from Land's End, England, the night of 7-8 November 1942. This was the first U.S. Army Airborne operation of the war and the longest Airborne invasion in history, 1,600 miles to Algeria, North Africa.

Our "package" followed by ship to Oran, Algeria and by train to Algiers where we were stationed at Maison Carrée. The Battalion had regrouped at Tafaraoui Airport and jumped again at Youks-les-Bains, Tunisia to capture Thelepte Airport. When the Battalion returned from Tunisia, Raff was promoted to Colonel and sent back to the US to form a new Regiment. We went west to Boufarik, Algeria (where Lily Pons was born) and then Oujda, French Morocco to be assigned to the new 5th Army.

While in Oujda, we went to Tlemden, Algeria to play baseball with the hospital team. In April 1943 after a game I was invited by a young boy to a Passover seder. When I got there the house was dark and no one was there. The boy apologized later for giving me wrong directions, as there was supposed to have been someone there to direct me to his grandmother's where the Seder was held.

In May 1943 after the North African campaign ended, the 82nd Airborne Division arrived at Oujda. Its first mission was to be the invasion of Sicily. The staff was all bent out of shape that we already had three operations under our belt before they arrived in North Africa (because of this, the Division "brass" took it out on us by refusing to let us attend the Bob Hope USO show when we got to Kairouan, Tunisia with the Division in June 1943).

After the invasion of Sicily, the nights of 9/10 July 1943, the Battalion followed the Division to Comiso and Licata, Sicily, but no mission had been assigned. LTC Yardley ordered me to bring up the administrative and supply "tail." Unknown to me, on the afternoon of 14 September 43, MG Matthew B. Ridgway, the Division commander, came to Battalion Hq and informed Yardley that night to block roads leading to the Salerno beachhead.

I went to Palermo, Sicily to arrange for an LST to bring my group to Naples (en route I ran into a classmate from UConn on the LST). When I reported to LTC William P. Yarborough at

FROM PARATROOPER TO PUBLIC DEFENDER

Piscinola around 1 October 1943 he appointed me Battalion Adjutant (Yardley had been wounded and captured on the Avellino jump).

We were sent to the Volturno Front and on 9 November 1943 made the assault on Mount Corno and Mount Croce just north of Venafro. LTC Yarborough led the assault and I was with him. I spent about forty days on the line on Mount Croce, serving as S-2 (Intelligence Officer), running patrols and taking prisoners. In December we were relieved to prepare for the Anzio-Nettuno beachhead operation.

On 22 January 1944 at 0400 hours we went over the side of H.M.S. Winchester Castle down cargo nets into British LCA (landing craft, assault) with no training, for the seaborne assault on Anzio beach. The Rangers (who had been with us at Venafro) had gone in at 0200 hours. I was in the lead LCA with LTC Yarborough and remember cracking a joke from Bill Mauldin's "Mud, Mules and Mountains" as we went in.

After hitting the beach I broke into a house left of the casino, through the house and right down the road to hit the Villa Borghese. Going to the second floor with Dick Fisco, we came to a closed door. Fisco blew the lock with his Thompson sub-machine gun and I charged in with my .45 pistol and a grenade – the room was empty, the Germans having bailed out the back window into the yard where Val Pierson's men got them.

The living room had been a headquarters and we found a map of all the mines on the beach that the engineers welcomed. On the sideboard was a bottle of Scotch and a Kodak Retina f 4.5 camera. SGT Leone wanted the Scotch so I took the camera, which I put to good use from there on. We were moving well along and got to Carano and received the incredible order from 6th Corps to "Stop and dig in!" We could have been in Rome that first day (the Germans were already evacuating). The enemy was able to occupy the hills around the beachhead and it was like shooting fish in a rain barrel. I was walking down a road and a German 105 mm howitzer crew spotted me and followed me with shell fire until I made it to cover.

FROM PARATROOPER TO PUBLIC DEFENDER

There were some 7,000 troops killed during the entire operation and when I came back from Europe with the 82nd Airborne Division I saw a white hospital ship moored to a pier in the Hudson River. It was the Blanche F. Sigmund, named for an Army nurse who was killed in an attack on the (well-marked) 93rd and 95th Evacuation Hospitals complex near the waterfront.

The 509th spearheaded the breakout from the beachhead through "houses #5 and #6" in May 1944 and we were sent to Lido di Roma on the west coast at Ostia, outside Rome. There was an electronics school there, built by the Fascist government and years later a client of mine in Hartford told me that he was there with the Italian army before the war. I sent some of the books we found to my Physics professor at UConn and he got a big kick from them.

We were staging for the Southern France invasion and made some practice jumps at Paestum. I met Joe Louis, the world's heavyweight champion who was in the area with an Army Air Corps USO unit. He would box with some of the troops, and knowing that none of them were anywhere near professional, he would "carry" them through a tough workout and make them look good, so they would not be embarrassed in front of their friends. He was a fine gentleman, very quiet, almost shy. I also met Irving Berlin, the composer, at a bar in Rome. He was in Italy presenting his famous show, "This is the Army."

The 509th Parachute Infantry Combat Team spearheaded the 1st Airborne Task Force invasion of Southern France, 14-15 August 1944 (Anvil-Dragoon). The unit jumped at Le Muy and St. Tropez. Faulty navigation led to a "stick" of seventeen troopers commanded by CPT Ralph R. Miller, Jr. of Youngstown, OH being lost when they dropped into the Golfe de St. Tropez and no bodies were ever recovered.

Yarborough refused to take me along on the Southern France mission and had me bring up the administrative and supply "tail" by ship from Naples. We conducted operations in the mountains above Nice at Lantosque and Piera Cava.

FROM PARATROOPER TO PUBLIC DEFENDER

After the Ardennes Campaign started 16 December 1944, we were sent to Belgium via horse portee trailer trucks a few days later, reporting to MG Maurice Rose, CG (commanding general) of the 3rd Armored Division, at Manhay. We were in combat operations on the Manhay-Erezee-Grandmenil highway, Sadzot (see extract from Breuer book: "Bloody Clash at Sadzot"), Soy, Hotton. We were then attached to the 7th Armored Division and fought at Koenigswald. The 509th captured St. Vith and ended up at Trois Ponts with seven officers and forty-three men still standing.

It had been desided at SHAEF (Supreme Headquarters of Allied Expeditionary Forces0 to disband all the small special units and reassign the personnel to the major Airborne units. In spite of orders that no enlisted personnel were to be reduced in rank as a result, many of our best non-commissioned officers were illegally reduced to private, mainly in the 82nd Airborne Division. This was in marked contrast to the fine treatment we received when attached to the 3rd Armored Division. On Christmas Day 1944 we were in combat in the Manhay, Erezee area and there were no rations. We were also short of supplies. Around noon a convoy of half-tracks from LTC Richardson's 33rd Armored Infantry came down the highway to our positions, delivering hot, roast stuffed turkey in insulated "Marmite' cans.

While we were conducting operations in the Ardennes we were assigned to XVIII Airborne Corps under command of LTC Matthew B. Ridgway, who had commanded the 82nd Airborne Division. We were in the Soy-Hotton area. Most of the Corps staff had come up from the 82nd Airborne Division and continued its discrimination against the 509th. COL Schellhammer, the Corps G-1, denied our C.O., MAJ Ed Tomasik, his well-earned promotion to LTC. (In October 1944, while we were in Southern France, LTC Yarborough was ordered back to the US to attend the U.S. Army Command & General Staff College at Fort Leavenworth. MAJ Tomasik assumed command and had more command time in combat than required for promotion to LTC. Schellhammer made sure Tomasik never

FROM PARATROOPER TO PUBLIC DEFENDER

received his promotion – in spite of which, Tomasik remained on active duty after the war and retired as a full 0-6 Colonel.)

I was one of a number of our officers, non-coms and men transferred to the 82nd Airborne Division. Most went to the 505th Parachute Infantry, one of the regiments. Most of the men were received very badly and treated very poorly. LTC Ireland, Division G-1, had lied to me about COL Ekman's having asked for me. However, Ekman assigned me as Assistant S-2, Intelligence Officer, and since the assigned S-2 was always off on some choice deal (i.e. running a DP camp or going to school in Paris), I was in fact the working S-2 to the end of the war.

With the 505th I went to the Rhine River where we captured the oil plant at Weseling before it could open and ran patrols across the river. I had occasion to test fire the new 75mm recoilless rifles across the Rhine. SGT Teague dropped a round through the vision slit of the pillbox on the third shot. The 75mm recoilless was a remarkable weapon and very accurate in the hands of SGT Teague.

I had occasion to conduct a homicide investigation there. We fished a dead Gestapo agent out of the river after a car ran our roadblock. There had been some shooting along the river the night before. After an investigation with one of my best interrogators, involving an adjacent French unit, German prostitutes, French forced laborers and some delicate inquires of the French, we concluded it was a revenge killing of the agent who had learned of the laborers being with the prostitutes and turning them in to the authorities. We recommended that the French keep their activities in their own sector and that was the end of it.

En route to the Elbe River we picked up an escaped German prisoner named Brahms (no relation to the composer). Since he could speak Russian I commandeered him as our German-Russian interpreter. We nearly got shot by panicky green troops of the 86th Infantry Division as we moved to the Elbe River.

The Division crossed the Elbe at Bleckede the morning of 30 April 1945. I was in the lead landing boat with the

Commanding Officer of the 505th Parachute Infantry, COL Ekman, under intense artillery fire. When we hit the other bank, MG James M. Gavin, commanding our 82nd Airborne Division, was there to meet us. He was wearing his beat-up old jump suit, carrying his own M-1 rifle. As always, he would go in first, never sending anyone where he would not go first.

In addition to heavy artillery fire, the Germans had mined the far river bank with mines containing seventy-five pounds of explosive that could be detonated three different ways. One of our trucks set off a mine with the pressure trip, sending the GMC 2½ ton six-wheel truck into the air. It came down just missing the driver's head.

We chased the enemy through the Bleckede, Alt Jabel, Ludwigslust and Vielank area, liberating the Wobbelin concentration camp at Ludwigslust. MG Gavin was so outraged when he saw this starvation camp that he made the populace carry the bodies into Ludwigslust and create a cemetery in the town square. My S-2 section captured the Nazi Colonel commanding the camp. When we searched his house (I got his 7.65 mm Mauser pistol) his wife was all bent out of shape that we were pulling the books off the library shelves. I had my interrogator tell her "if this Nazi pig doesn't shut up, I'll cut her damned throat". We found a book of the 1936 Olympics that included Ivan Fuqua's triumph in track and field. (Ivan had become track coach at the University of Connecticut, and I sent him the book).

On May 3, 1945 the German XXI Army surrendered to the 82nd Airborne Division at Ludwigslust. It was very satisfying to have the job of taking one of the German generals, along with some of his staff, to the P.O.W. compound. I crowded them into my jeep and dropped them off at the prisoner of war area.

After returning to Sissonne, France we were prepared for occupation duty in Berlin. We entered Berlin early in the summer and set up headquarters in the Schlachtensee area. I was transferred to serve as Regimental Personnel Officer and had the opportunity to spend a week in the Southern France R&R area. I spent a week at a luxury hotel (most probably the California in

Cannes). It was an interesting trip back to Berlin, as the pilot took me forward and I was in the co-pilot seat all the way.

I was able to attend services for the High Holy Days of Rosh Hashanah and Yom Kippur. The Military Chaplain of the Berlin District was a rabbi and he reopened and re-consecrated the principal Synagogue in Berlin. This had been closed and desecrated when the Nazis came to power. The chaplain found out I was a Kohane, a direct descendant of Aaron, the brother of Moses, designating me as a High Priest of Israel. This entitled me to give the first blessing at the reading of the Torah, the sacred scroll.

At the service, over half the congregation was comprised of Soviet soldiers, with the soft garrison cap, the batty blouse and the boots. They carried worn prayer books, long hidden from the Soviet authorities. It was an indescribable feeling to be on the pulpit, giving the first blessing at the first service since the Nazis had closed the Synagogue. (I felt like Judah Maccabee after he had driven the Syrians and Greeks from the Land of Israel.

One of my vivid recollections of the Anzio beach-head operation concerns an arrogant Nazi pilot who was shot down over the beach-head. We interrogated him to learn the location of his airfield in order to have the (then) Army Air Corps destroy it. He was very stubborn until I told my interrogator to advise the pilot who and what I was. He told the pilot (as best as I can reproduce the language): "Der Oberleutnant ist ein Jude". The pilot turned the color of dirty ashes and caved in, giving us the needed information.

Probably the funniest story I recall is about the Thanksgiving turkeys. Due to a miscalculation in 1942 about how long the North African campaign would last, the supply system came up short and we were authorized to obtain turkeys from the local economy, at sixty pounds per hundred men and pay sixty cents a pound. I arranged with a local entrepreneur to raise the turkeys. The day before Thanksgiving he came to me stating that the chief of police in Sattarno (sic) had confiscated the turkeys on the claim they were being raised for the black market, and telling me they were "just down the road." I took off with him in his alcohol burning truck, with only a soft cap, fatigue coveralls, a GI raincoat, "boondocker" work shoes and carrying my Colt .45.

After a long haul he pointed to a road marker, saying "There it is!" It read St. Arnaud 240 km. We got there late at night after many stops to clean out the carburetor and getting past the railroad barriers. The chief apologized to me, but he had turned my turkeys over to the British at Constantine, so they were lost.

I spent the night at a local café drinking hot, sweet Turkish coffee (it was like a Hollywood casting call with French Foreign Legion soldiers, Arab Goumiers with tarbooshes (a green fez) and miscellaneous French soldiers and Arab civilians). I hitched a ride back to Maison Carrée with a very suspicious Army chaplain in a broken down Army vehicle. He kept a beady eye on me until we arrived and the sentry saluted me in.

The turkeys arrived for Christmas and we served hot, roast stuffed turkey to the whole Battalion. That night I was censoring mail, and one young trooper wrote home to his mother: "Mom, to-day we had roast stuffed turkey. I hate roast stuffed turkey!" Years later my daughters used this story as the basis of respective high school themes.

I stayed in the Army Reserve after coming home with the 82nd Airborne Division (my regiment, the 505th Parachute Infantry, led the Victory Parade up Fifth Avenue in January 1946). I went to UConn Law School on the GI Bill, served seventeen years in the 411th Civil Affairs Company, West Hartford, the last eight years as Commanding Officer. When I was promoted to Colonel, LTG Yarborough had me assigned to OACSI G-2 at the Pentagon, where I worked with DIA.

In 1972 I was retired after thirty-four years of service. OACSI awarded me the Legion of Merit and I had received the Bronze Star Medal (V) with Oakleaf Cluster, Army Commendation Medal, European-African-Middle Eastern Service Medal with nine campaign stars and invasion arrowhead, Victory Medal, Army of Occupation Medal, Medal of French Liberation and Reserve Service Medal. With the 509th I was awarded the Presidential Unit Citation with two Oakleaf Clusters for actions at Anzio and the Ardennes and with the 505th for action in Germany. I earned the Combat Infantryman Badge and Parachute Qualification Badge.

Morton N. Katz
COL-AUS (ret)

Addendum: While it may seem that we spent a lot of time pulling off stunts and getting away with various things, we did manage to do the things we were getting paid for. However, one more "goof-off" stunt comes to mind and I can't resist sharing it.

The 82nd Airborne left Berlin, Germany in December 1945. (COL. Ekman tried to take his Mercedes-Benz staff car with him. He got as far as Le Havre and was not allowed to load the car on the cross-Channel boat. It went back to Berlin with the driver of the Commander who succeeded Ekman.)

The Division staff was not too concerned with creature comforts for the troops and planned an overnight bivouac for the units between Berlin and Camp Oklahoma City at Rheims, France on an open, cold, wet hillside in Belgium. One of my men told me he knew a great restaurant in Belgium where we could get a great steak dinner, wine, Belgian pastries and hang out until dawn. We faked a breakdown of our ¾ ton command car and cut off to the restaurant.

It was just great and when we left in the morning the fog was so thick it could be cut with a knife. Two men with flashlights draped themselves over the big front fenders to locate the road. We pulled into Camp Oklahoma City and reported to MAJ Wagner, the Regimental S-4 (Supply). We mentioned the "breakdown" and he came back with a word I shall not repeat. However, nothing happened and we got away with it. Years later I ran into Wagner (now LTC Wagner) when I was at the Advanced Course of The Infantry School at Fort Benning. He invited me to his on-post quarters for dinner and I asked him if he believed the breakdown story. He looked at me and responded: "I wouldn't believe you no-good so and sos for anything."

FROM PARATROOPER TO PUBLIC DEFENDER

Going back to Ekman's car, my C.O. in the 509th found Sidney Chaplin's 1936 Cord in a garage under a hotel in Nice. He had to leave it behind in 1940 when he left ahead of the Nazis. We used it for a few months and it broke our hearts to have to leave it behind when we went north to Villers-Cotterets. It was some car!

I'll quit and save the story of the courts-martial records I destroyed when we left Oklahoma City for Le Havre.

- - - - -
-

Bibliography

Bennett, Lowell. *Assignment to Nowhere (The Battle for Tunisia)*. New York: Vanguard Press, 1953, pp. 48-53, 63-66, ch. 5.

Blumenson, Martin, *Salerno to Cassino*. United States Army in World War II. Washington: Government Printing Office, 1969.

Carvey, James B. "Faid Pass," *Infantry Journal*, LV (September 1944, pp. 8-13.

Historical Section, War Department. *Anzio Beachhead*. American Forces in Action Series. Washington: Government Printing Office, 1947.

From the Volturno to the Winter Line. American Forces in Action Series. Washington: Government Printing Office, 1944.

Salerno: American Operations from the Beaches to the Volturno. American Forces in Action Series. Washington: Government Printing Office, 1945.

Howe, George F. *Northwest Africa: Seizing the Initiative in the West*. United States Army in World War II. Washington: Government Printing Office, 1957.

Hutton, Bud. "Nice Kids, Our Daredevils." *The New York Times Magazine* (3 January 1943). P. 4

Life, XV (18 January 1943) pp. 30-31 (photographs)

Parachute Battalion. Baton Rouge: Army and Navy Publishing Company, 1942.

Raff, Edson Duncan. *We jumped to Fight*. New York: Eagle Books, 1944.

Sheehan, Fred. *Anzio*. Norman: University of Oklahoma Press, 1964.

Wharton, Don. "Dan DeLeo: Paratrooper in Tunisia." *Look,* VII (9 July 1943) p. 42

"Paratroop Doctor Saves Lives in Desert Hell. *Look*. VII (13 July 1943) p. 52

Yarborough, William P. "House Party in Jerryland." *The Infantry Journal,* LV (July 1944) pp, 8-15.

Made in the USA
Middletown, DE
28 February 2023